PHalarope Books

PHalarope Books are designed specifically for the amateur naturalist. These volumes represent excellence in natural history publishing. Each book in the PHalarope series is based on a nature course or program at the college or adult education level or is sponsored by a museum or nature center. Each PHalarope Book reflects the author's teaching ability as well as writing ability.

BOOKS IN THE SERIES

The Curious Naturalist
JOHN MITCHELL and THE MASSACHUSETTS AUDUBON SOCIETY

The Amateur Naturalist's Handbook
VINSON BROWN

Outdoor Education: A Manual for Teaching in Nature's Classroom
MICHAEL LINK, Director,
Northwoods Audubon Center, Minnesota

Nature Photography: A Guide to Better Outdoor Pictures
STAN OSOLINSKI

Nature Drawing: A Tool for Learning
CLARE WALKER LESLIE

Nature with Children of All Ages: Activities and Adventures for Exploring, Learning, and Enjoying the World around Us
EDITH SISSON, THE MASSACHUSETTS AUDUBON SOCIETY

The Wildlife Observer's Guidebook
CHARLES E. ROTH, THE MASSACHUSETTS AUDUBON SOCIETY

A Complete Manual of Amateur Astronomy: Tools and Techniques for Astronomical Observations
P. CLAY SHERROD with THOMAS L. KOED

Michael Link is Director of the Northwoods Audubon Center in Sandstone, Minnesota. He has written numerous books and professional journal articles and has backpacked, canoed, and hiked throughout the North American continent.

Michael Link

OUTDOOR EDUCATION

A Manual for Teaching in Nature's Classroom

A SPECTRUM BOOK

Prentice-Hall, Inc., Englewood Cliffs, New Jersey 07632

Library of Congress Cataloging in Publication Data

Link, Mike.
    Outdoor education.

    (A Spectrum Book) (A PHalarope Book)
    Bibliography: p.
    1. Outdoor education—Handbooks, manuals, etc.
2. Nature study—Handbooks, manuals, etc.   I. Title.
LB1047.L56   371.3′8   81-10546
                                      AACR2

ISBN 0-13-645028-8

ISBN 0-13-645010-5 {PBK.}

This book is based on the publication *Nature's Classroom: A Manual
for Teaching Outdoor Education* by Michael Link, copyright 1978 by the
National Audubon Society, 950 Third Avenue, New York, New York 10022.
© 1981 by Prentice-Hall, Inc., Englewood Cliffs, New Jersey 07632.

10   9   8   7   6   5   4   3

Editorial/production supervision
and interior design by Kimberly Mazur
Art production by Mary Greey
Manufacturing buyer: Cathie Lenard

Prentice-Hall International, Inc., *London*
Prentice-Hall of Australia Pty. Limited, *Sydney*
Prentice-Hall of Canada, Ltd., *Toronto*
Prentice-Hall of India Private Limited, *New Delhi*
Prentice-Hall of Japan, Inc., *Tokyo*
Prentice-Hall of Southeast Asia Pte. Ltd., *Singapore*
Whitehall Books Limited, *Wellington, New Zealand*

Contents

Preface

Outdoor education demands virtuosity. There is no single definition of outdoor education, nor is there an individual area of study that
is sufficient to prepare students for all the possible applications of
their chosen profession.

The intent of this book is to emphasize the need for an ecological
philosophy and to introduce the student to a variety of possible
applications of their interest.

The ultimate success of any individual will be the blending of
their interests and skills with a program and an audience. Creativity,
imagination, and determination are the ingredients of success. No
two outdoor education people will ever be the same, nor will their
program.

This book covers a diversity of activities and ideas. If properly
blended with enthusiasm, experience, and personal skill, it will help
the reader become a successful outdoor educator.

ACKNOWLEDGMENTS

Many people and organizations cooperated to make this book possible. I would like to thank: Jane Link, for photographs, typing, and constructive criticism; Quarry Hill, Lowry, Eastman, and Wood Lake Nature Centers, and the Deep-Portage Conservation Reserve, for photos and pertinent information; Craig R. Borck, photographer for the St. Paul, Minnesota, newspapers and a good personal friend, for some of his photographs; David J. Eagan, a former student and intern at Northwoods, for his cartoon drawings. Northwoods Audubon Center, where I have had the opportunity to put into practice the ideas that I discuss in the text.

And, finally, I extend my thanks to God for the gift of nature.

The quotation on page 28 by Professor John Kennedy is used by permission of John Kennedy, Scarborough College, Toronto, Canada.

The excerpt from *A Continuous Harmony*, by Wendell Berry, is used by permission of Harcourt Brace Jovanovich.

The excerpt from *The Mountain People*, by Colin Turnbull, is used by permission of Simon and Schuster, New York.

The excerpt from *Pilgrim at Tinker Creek*, by Annie Dillard, copyright © 1974 by Annie Dillard. Reprinted by permission of Harper & Row, Publishers, Inc.

Grazing, the Minnesota Wild Eater's Food Book, by Mike Link, is published by Voyageur Press, Bloomington, Minnesota.

Excerpts from *How to Talk to Birds*, by Richard C. Davids, and *Reflections from the North Country*, by Sigurd F. Olson, illustrated by Leslie Kouba, are used by permission of Alfred A. Knopf, Inc.

Black Elk Speaks, by John G. Neihardt, published by Simon and Schuster and the Nebraska Press. Copyright 1932, 1961 by John Neihardt.

The excerpt from *The Unexpected Universe*, by Loren Eiseley, is used by permission of Harcourt Brace Jovanovich and Victor Gollancz, Ltd.

The excerpt from "Come Back Smiling," by Cliff Jacobson, copyright © Voyager Publications Inc. 1980. Reprinted with permission from April/May 1980 Canoe magazine, 131 E. Murray St., Fort Wayne, IN 46803.

The excerpt from *Lives of the Hunted*, by Ernest Thompson Seton, is used by permission of Charles Scribner's Sons.

The excerpt from *The Sense of Wonder*, by Rachel Carson, copyright © 1956 Rachel L. Carson. Reprinted by permission of Harper & Row, Publishers, Inc.

The excerpt from Loren Eiseley, *The Innocent Assassins, New Poems* copyright © 1973 by Loren Eiseley. (New York: Charles Scribner's Sons, 1973). Reprinted with the permission of Charles Scribner's Sons.

Excerpts on pages 8 (two excerpts), 138, and 194 from *A Sand County Almanac with other essays on conservation from Round River* by Aldo Leopold, copyright © 1949, 1953, 1966, renewed 1977, 1981 by Oxford University Press, Inc. Reprinted by permission.

I would like to dedicate this book to the following two men:

To Sigurd Olson: No man has stood taller as an inspiration and a model. He is the man of the North Country. He is a man who loves the land, learns its secrets, and fights for its preservation.

To Bert Link: He is my grandfather, and I love him.

One

Outdoor Inspiration

Surely there is something in the unruffled calm of nature that
overawes our little anxieties and doubts: the sight of the deep-blue
sky, and the clustering stars above, seem to impart a quiet to the
mind.

JONATHAN EDWARDS
American Theologian 1703-1758

Going outside does not mean that the regular classroom is not a vital
center for learning. Taking a class outside means extending the
school's sphere of influence. To go outside means to take learning and
apply it to the playground, the woods, the lakeshore, the lawn, and
the city streets.

The outdoor world is exciting, inspiring, and constantly changing. The mysteries to be solved and the beauty to be found are com-
plementary, not conflicting, to classroom learning. Mark Twain's
classic characters, Huck Finn and Tom Sawyer, may not have represented the ideal students, but they did represent the lure of the
woods, caves and rivers—those great unknown places—and who
could argue that Huck and Tom did not learn from their outdoor
adventures? How much more could they have learned if their school
had given them directions to explore nature?

In the outdoors we find a great reservoir of truth and constancy.
Thoreau wrote:

The wilderness is near as well as dear to every man. Even the oldest villages are indebted to the border of wild wood which surrounds them, more than to the gardens of men. There is something indescribably inspiring and beautiful in the aspect of the forest skirting and occasionally jutting into the midst of new towns, which, like the sand-heaps of fresh fox-burrows, have sprung up in their midst. The very uprightness of the pines and maples asserts the ancient rectitude and vigor of nature. Our lives need the relief of such a background, where the pine flourishes and the jay still screams.

The natural world has inspired not only writers and philosophers. Painters Thomas Cole, John James Audubon, Catesby, and Fuertes, and photographers Moran, Adams, Porter, and Blacklock found nature to be the perfect subject for their artistic expression.

The American Indians expressed many feelings for nature in their songs. Their lives were attuned to the rhythm of nature, and, consequently, the rhythm of their songs was more important than the words, reflecting the cycles of nature. In the "Horse Dance," Black Elk begins his song with, "Father, paint the earth on me." Music and art, human and earth, were one.

The Mississippi River may have changed since Tom Sawyer's time, but it is richer for the history that it embraces

Composers, too, were affected by the world of nature. Schubert and Beethoven both found the Vienna woods, the Wienerwald, to be the spiritual home of the music and poetry of their age. Beethoven looked out on the Wienerwald as it stretched its forested fingers to the Alps and declared, "Nobody can love this landscape as much as I."

Vivaldi's "The Four Seasons," Grofé's "Grand Canyon Suite," and hundreds of other compositions have been written to capture the beauty of nature in sound. Ballad and folk singers have continued this tradition of "man-nature-sound" right into the present with singers like Pete Seeger and John Denver.

The charm and beauty of the natural world act as a magnet to humans. Thousands of people pour into the woods each weekend and on vacations, looking for something special, something they cannot find at home. I have been turned away from the back country of the Great Smoky Mountains National Park because a quarter of a million people were already out there.

Outdoor education's challenge is to provide inspiration, to encourage observation, to develop ethical values, and to gain a perspective on the human role in the mechanism called Earth.

For too long we have allowed bells, clocks, and schedules to rule education. Although beneficial at times, such tools often limit the learning experience for the student. The outdoors does not conform to a rigid schedule. Outdoor education may necessitate team teaching, an overlap with other subjects, appeals to an administration and school board, and lots of preliminary headaches, but it is worth it. As a teacher your job is to provide the best educational experience that you can give, and that may take some effort.

A classroom without walls contrasts with a teacher's formal training and creates a picture of unbridled behavior problems, students disappearing over the horizon in defiance, and a general nightmare of unanswerable questions and "uncatchable" kids. The result is that most students receive formal education indoors and must then apply it to the outside world on their own. This type of teaching subtly tells students that they learn when they are inside the classroom and stop learning when they are outside of it. School divides life into learning time and non-learning time, when actually the essence of life itself is constant learning.

Perhaps one of the greatest lessons of the outdoor classroom is this: we *can* learn everywhere and we can learn with and without books. We can apply what we read and we can go beyond it. Outdoor education does not fit easily into preconceived notions; it is widespread in scope and far-reaching in audience.

One of the challenges for environmental education is the measuring of our position in the scales of earthly balance. We must learn our place in the gradual movements of geology and astronomy; we must see our relationship with other living organisms; and we must realize the effect that we have on one another.

We must delve beyond the question "What good is it for me?" to an understanding of the complexities of earth's delicate web of life. It is difficult to predict the consequences of any of our actions. Too often we think of the results of our actions in terms of decades, yet the people of the 1970s who have suffered the effects of radiation at Love Canal and the oppressive smog in Los Angeles know firsthand the danger inherent in human greed.

Environmental educators are futurists. We seek a positive condition for future life. Our outdoor classroom can be any blank spot that is available to us. Even the most abused landscape has a message to share and, in the end, the sharing will provide rewards that exceed the effort.

I enjoyed going to the Northwoods and the making of maple syrup. The part I liked best was when you showed us how the Indians used to make maple syrup.

The kaleidoscope of natural environments includes the stark and dramatic, such as the Badlands of South Dakota.

After the trip I went home and tried to make some syrup on my own.
It wasn't very easy doing it with a big spike and a hammer. The next
day I put up seven cans. Three days later I collected it all. Would
you believe I got only one quart with the water in it? About a week
later I had one lard can full. My mother boiled it down and got one
cup without the water. That night I got all my cans and put them
back on the trees. This time I got more than a cup of syrup. On April
20th we got permission to tap the trees of Bork's tree farm which is
about a mile from our place. We started right after school Thurs-
day. We tapped one tree and the sap came squirting out at us. I'm
anxious to find out how much syrup I got. I couldn't make the kind
of spouts you made, so I'm using copper tubing. (Letter from
student, Northwoods Audubon Center)

Many elementary and secondary schools have environmental sites
that offer potential studies for all grades and disciplines. The use of
such a site, however, should not be limited to classtime. Use students
for the planning, development, and maintenance of the site. Involve
clubs, parents, local gardeners, bird watchers, and professionals. This
participation will add a great deal to the learning process.

Indoor, in-class subjects can be greatly enhanced by outdoor
studies. Sometimes classroom programs place too much emphasis on
other places. For example, if a volcano study emphasizes Kilauea,
Hawaii, the student in Wisconsin who never travels will not comprehend the impact of the study. There are volcanic rocks in Wisconsin and perhaps by touching one, the student will comprehend more
fully, and perhaps more enthusiastically, one of the complexities in
our world.

An American history teacher might take a class to a hilly area
and walk silently from a valley to the top of a ridge where the woods
and lakes and ponds stretch out to the horizon. When the class pauses
to capture the view, the teacher might say with a sweeping stroke of
the arm, "This is why people moved west. This is the source for their
inspiration." They might do nothing else that day, or they might sit
and discuss the western expansion, or they might move out and map
an unknown area just as early adventurers had done.

The outdoor classroom can be an individual learning area too.
Observations of home bird feeders, squirrel behavior, flowers, trees,
weather, or a hundred different phenomena can be extra credit or
independent study material. Even the maintenance of bird feeders on
a school site can be an exciting and important responsibility to a grade
school student.

Public lands are administered by agencies that often have
printed bird lists, maps, and general information brochures. There are

trails, plants, wildlife, historic sites, and personnel to guide you. Use state wildlife refuges, parks and forests, as well as federal parks, forests, grasslands, refuges, monuments, dam sites, and historic sites. Visit city parks, zoos, arboretums, gardens, and sanctuaries. Contact the National Audubon Society and The Nature Conservancy for information on their sanctuaries.

Visit some of the nearly one thousand nature centers in the United States and participate in their programs. Utilize their naturalists, trails, buildings, and materials. They often have classes for adults and college students, as well as programs for school classes. One advantage of the nature center is the introduction of a new element: the outside expert.

"When I got to hold the pail, I was glad."

"I had a good time. I let my Dad taste the maple sap. He said that our maple sap was better than your maple sap."

"Thank you for a most fun day at Northwoods. I had so much fun and learned so much. I like the bee's honey too and you looked funny with that hat and net over your head. Come and visit us at school sometime."

The best procedure to follow in planning a visit to a nature center is to contact the center first and arrange to see the brochure that describes the center's activities. Make an appointment to discuss what can be done with your group. Prepare for this program-developing session by having the following information ready for the meeting:

1. Group size and age. Number of leaders.
2. Specific background interests.
3. Handicaps of the group.
4. What do you expect to accomplish at the nature center that you cannot do someplace else?

"When I got to hold the pail I was glad."
COURTESY DAVID J. EAGAN

5. Time available for preparation, field session, and follow-up.
6. Help needed in terms of materials, workforce, and audio-visual for preparation and follow-up.

The nature center personnel should be able to provide ideas for meeting your goals, suggestions for materials and preparation needs, and their available staff and time.

Some nature centers provide only resident programs, which allow for more intensive studies and more teacher-student rapport than short courses. Different activities build upon one another and develop deeper lessons and lifetime memories.

> Thanks a lot for everything. Cross country skiing, dishwashing, snowshoeing, bread baking, lumberjacking, snowshowering in the morning, and lots of laughter and happiness together with our United Nations and you. You three big kids really taught me how to love nature and appreciate our ground as it is.
>
> MARIO: American Field Service Student
> Sao Paulo, Brazil

Many American Camping Association summer camps have naturalists that are trained through the ACA Ecological Training Program; some of these camps are open year round or may allow their grounds to be used. The National Audubon Society and the National Wildlife Federation also offer summer study sessions.

An outdoor study site does not have to be a pristine wilderness. In fact, much can be learned from an area that is heavily used. What is missing and why tells a great deal about human impact.

We are faced with a problem of human encroachment that threatens in the most innocuous ways to destroy the values we love, and we are part of this human paradox. We lack a knowledge of how to be outdoors without loving it to death. We live by the laws of the wilds, yet we defy those wilds and seek to overcome those laws.

Aldo Leopold wrote, "The man who cannot enjoy his leisure is

The outdoor classroom is a contrast to formal teaching.

ignorant, though his degrees exhaust the alphabet, and the man who does enjoy his leisure is to some extent educated, though he has never seen the inside of a school."

Humans are substituting machines for muscles, consuming resources to appreciate resources. Our lands are measured in dollars instead of aesthetics. Lake homes dot the north and destroy the land that the owners came to enjoy. Massive veins of concrete, blacktop, and steel wind through the wilds, laying beneath them millions of acres of natural habitats so that people might get closer to the wilds.

We, as a species, are too often unwilling to pay the price to find the values we seek. We need to know the rhythm of the hike, the glide of the canoe, and the cross country ski, but even more important, we need to place a value on those things we may never see, simply because they are there.

Aldo Leopold stated:

> Poor land may be rich country, and vice versa. Only economists mistake physical opulence for riches. Country may be rich despite a conspicuous poverty of physical endowment, and its quality may not be apparent at first glance nor at all times.
>
> ---
>
> In country, as in people, a plain exterior often conceals hidden riches, to perceive which requires much living with. Nothing is more monotonous than the juniper foothills, until some veteran of a

An area need not be void of people to be a good natural history area.

thousand summers, laden blue with berries, explodes in a blue burst of chattering jays. The drab sogginess of a March cornfield, saluted by one honker from the sky, is drab no more.

No one can list all the reasons that people have for going outside, but frequently it is to escape the pressures of their daily lives. Many seek excitement in outdoor adventure, some seek discovery in bird watching and rock picking. Some people just want to relax; others want to push themselves.

Why do people visit nature centers? Why should classes go outside? The answers vary.

One Philadelphia naturalist says that groups visit because it is a day off for the teacher, a field trip, and fun for the kids. The goals of his center's staff are to compensate for urban backgrounds, recognizing and diminishing fears by acclimatization and fun. The staff wants children to have an enjoyable time learning how life works. Natural areas can be as threatening to inner city kids as Tarzan jungles; students must visit wild places to learn otherwise.

A Minnesota teacher believes the outdoors is a link with reality. He said, "We need to realize that the world consists of more than ideas and theory. It has three dimensions. Sometimes learning reaches a point where the student cannot paint the appropriate picture in his mind without some tangible experience."

We are in need of the wilds or we would not be experiencing weekly human migrations. But we are also destroying our world. In the early 1970s Roderick Nash stated that we had the same amount of land preserved in wilderness as we had covered with pavement. We have continued to pave since then.

Outdoor educators are missionaries of the wild. Those of us who choose to speak for the animals, plants, rocks, waters, and ecologically sound human communities have the most fantastic array of assets ever, including human intelligence, a sense of excitement and adventure, and curiosity.

> The highest function of the teacher consists not so much in imparting knowledge as in stimulating the pupil in its love and pursuit. To know how to suggest is the art of teaching.
>
> H. H. AMIEL, Swiss philosopher
> 1821-1881

All naturalists should maintain the curiosity, enthusiasm, and insatiable thirst for knowledge that they have when they enter this world. In 1908 Anna Botsford Comstock wrote:

Nature-study is, despite all discussions and perversions, a study of nature; it consists of simple, truthful observations that may, like beads on a string, finally be threaded upon the understanding and thus held together as a logical and harmonious whole. Therefore, the object of the nature-study teacher should be to cultivate in the children powers of accurate observation and to build up within them, understanding.

In addition, she stated,

Nature-study is perfectly good science within its limits, but it is not meant to be more profound or comprehensive than the capabilities of the child's mind.

None of us lives more than 125 years in this world that counts its age in millions and billions of years. We are less than one second in the earth's day, so we have no right to be smug or arrogant. We entered the world as a species at 10:30 P.M. on the last day of the earth's year and developed science and technology as the clock swept past midnight. As an individual we are a blur in time, yet we have seen air and water

We are but a fleeting second in the waves of time—do we have the right to damage the future in that time?

fouled; we have seen several hundred species of animals become extinct; and we have watched our resources dwindle to shortage proportions. Much devastation can be caused by even one person. We can do only so much, but we must do what we can, for survival is the responsibility of every individual of every species.

Are our efforts as educators fruitful? We cannot always measure our results immediately. The people we see at our center are influenced by parents, contemporaries, teachers, and media, to name just a few factors. Our hope is to modify human decisions so that we do not destroy the earth or its ability to sustain life.

Two

Who Are You Going to Teach?

I suspect that the child plucks its first flower with an insight into its beauty and significance which the subsequent botanist never retains.

THOREAU

Within each community there are distinct groups of individuals with different interests and capabilities. Each is a potential audience for environmental education, but each demands an understanding of its expectations and limitations. The instructor's job involves more than the preparation of materials: it demands preparation for the individuals.

Following are some basic guidelines for teaching various groups. Often a project or idea set forth for one age group is applicable to other age groups as well.

Pre-Schoolers. Usually, the preschool teacher does not present a formal educational program but rather acts as a guide for the children's play activities. One direction for an environmental education program in this age bracket is to capitalize on the child's love of play. Playing is an activity performed by young dogs, chimps, birds, wolves, and other wild animals; it is a necessary part of the maturation

Let the students make their own discoveries.

process. Wild animals learn the techniques of hunt and defense through play. Play is a pleasurable way to practice for the more demanding times of life.

Many modern educators tend to relegate play to "filler" times, such as between school periods, which can do an injustice to the learning process.

An organization called The New Games Foundation (P.O. Box 7901, San Francisco, California) has published *The New Games Book* with many creative, minimal-competition activities. This book is useful for all ages, but preschool is the time to begin.

Make learning in the outdoors both fun and fascinating. Familiar activities can be moved to an outdoor environment: Play hide and seek, but make it an exercise in camouflage. Explain to the children that animals hide for protection, not for fun. Show them different types of camouflage that animals use and have them adopt one of the camouflage methods as the way that they will try. *Animal Camouflage* by Dorothy Shuttlesworth (The Natural History Press) is a good picture book to use for examples.

The students might use make-up, create costumes, or look for specific hiding spots. The seekers should also be limited. They should be looking for specific students who represent their prey, and they should be limited in the way that they can look. They could be restricted to a trail and have to see their prey from a distance. Perhaps they should have blinders on, because their eyes don't move in their sockets, or they should wear glasses that would limit their color range. Experiment with ideas.

A variation of "pom-pom pull away" can be played to teach about predator and prey.

Choose one person to be a bird and the remainder of the students to be insects. Have the insects line up along the margin of the playing field with their object to be getting to the other side without being caught by the bird.

As he or she moves between lines, the bird captures the insects by tagging them. The insects immediately become birds and help to capture more insects. They become a metaphor for a successful bird which is capable of multiplying only because it has the food to survive. They must capture an insect each round, or they must sit down or revert back to being insects. This represents starvation and death. If they become an insect it is because the death of the bird feeds an insect.

There should be some discussion about what has happened. For example, is it possible to maintain more predators than prey? Like all games, this can be used with older groups and the discussion can become more involved as age increases.

Kindergarten. This is a preparatory period in which children are taught to acquire the skills and attitudes that will be a part of their future schooling.

The outdoor classroom experience at this stage helps establish the fact that learning can take place in many contexts. Make the experience short and a mixture of fact and fun. Introduce frequent but short activities, and take toilet and cookie breaks.

Learn with magnifying glasses and rulers. Measure and find plants and animals that are less than one inch or one centimeter tall. Make a group terrarium that can be brought into the classroom, or make an ant farm (see chapter 4).

Use injured animals as teaching tools when they are available. Children of this age are captivated by live animals. Invite a bird bander to the class or visit a bander in the field, yard or woods to watch the bird banding activity.

Beware of the students' ability to take over the class. They all want the recognition that comes from telling a story, and if you let them get started, the class will evolve into a tall tale contest.

Eastman Nature Center in Minnesota (Hennepin County Park Reserve District) uses puppets as an introductory activity for kindergarten and grades that follow. Kids are fascinated by the motion of the colorful animals. The puppets hold the attention of the students for longer periods of time than an adult could. Children will listen with greater interest and with greater patience to the puppet.

Eastman Nature Center has found other benefits too. Puppetry, they say, helps develop spontaneous speech; improves enunciation and projection; increases oral reading skills with use of scripts; develops coordination; increases students' self-confidence and personal satisfaction; acts as an emotional release; and helps lead students to an interest in an academic area. The Center has provided the following information for people interested in puppetry.

PUPPETEERING BY EASTMAN NATURE CENTER

Special Effects for Sound and Action

1. Thunder: Bend a heavy sheet of cardboard or a piece of tin violently back and forth so that it moves in waves.
2. Rain: Sprinkle dried peas or rice into a metal baking dish or roll marbles around in a cardboard carton.
3. Wind: Use human sound effects or pull a smooth stick across a tightly stretched piece of silky material.
4. Galloping horse: Alternately and rhythmically tap two small wooden blocks or strike upside down cups on a wooden floor or board.
5. Gurgling stream or boiling liquid: Put a straw into a cup of water and blow hard.
6. Mist, fog, or smoke: Blow corn starch or baking soda through a narrow tube by squeezing a container filled with this that is attached to one end. Dry ice can be sprinkled with water just prior to the time for the special effect. A fire extinguisher can be let off for a few seconds at a time.
7. Waves in the ocean: Painted muslin or silky material can be held at either end and moved.
8. Fire: Create dancing shadows in front of a red light by placing something that moves in front. Streamers can be placed on the front side of a fan at low speed.
9. Flash of light (lightning): Use flash attachment from a camera; flick stage lights on and off quickly.
10. Wilting flower: Make stem using curtain spring; insert rod, then, when wilting is to take place, pull rod out slightly.
11. Snow or magic dust: Throw up soap flakes or paper confetti.

12. Balloons and party blowers: Affix balloon or blower to mouth of puppet with a hidden plastic hose that extends to the puppeteer's mouth. This method can be adapted for other clever uses, for example, balloon can be used to show chest breathing in and out, or stomach getting larger and larger.

Movement Techniques

Children will enjoy doing puppet motions as a group, each operating a puppet under the direction of an adult, or in response to the mood represented by music, or to actions in a story. Here are some suggested movements:

1. Walking: leisurely, hurriedly, with a limp
2. Running: like a jogger, like a runner in a race, with an occasional leap
3. Hopping or jumping: as if playing hopscotch or jumprope, or like a rabbit
4. Skipping or dancing: as to rock and roll, a waltz, or a Latin beat
5. Coughing, hiccuping, or sneezing
6. Waving good-bye, rubbing a hungry stomach, or playing patty-cake
7. Showing sadness, disgust, delight, surprise, anger, fear, drowsiness, shame, rejection, fatigue, amusement, or anticipation

Manipulation

1. The operator should look at the puppet in order to keep it at the correct height (particularly in relation to any other puppets on stage), prevent it from losing good posture and eye contact with other puppets and the audience, and in general operate it convincingly.

2. A puppeteer should maintain a consistent style of movement for each puppet character. Bigger characters tend to move more ponderously than smaller ones. A dancer should dance, not simply bounce around on the stage. There should be contrast in the ways that different character types move.

3. Puppets should move when they speak, using broad, exaggerated motions that communicate the story ideas clearly, eliminating the need for extensive dialogue. Even so, it is sometimes necessary to include a statement about the action in the story. This can occur in the narration or within the response of another puppet: "Did you get hurt when you tripped over that rock?'', instead of simply, "Did you get hurt?''.

4. The puppets should make use of all parts of the stage. They can go in and out of doors, peer through windows, and appear at different levels, around corners, from behind doors, or over edges. Sometimes it is appropriate to have a puppet come out in front of a stage as is commonly done with marionettes or story-telling puppets.

5. Puppet movements can become more clearly defined by having a puppet anticipate an action, such as by briefly stepping back before moving forward. This action is particularly important after a puppet has been still for a moment.

6. Puppets should enter and exit from the sides or through backdrop and scenery openings rather than popping up and down. However, some performance styles and puppet characters can and even should use different ways to enter and exit. For example, a puppet can effectively convey the idea of climbing stairs as it comes up into view.

Some good reference books on puppetry are *Hand and Rod Puppets*, by Hansjurgen Fettig; *Complete Book of Puppetry*, by David Currel (both from Boston Plays, Inc.); and *The Magic of Puppetry*, by Peggy Davison Jenkins (a Prentice-Hall Spectrum Book).

Use other games with kindergarten children too, but make them simple variations of childhood games with a natural history slant. Play "Captain, May I?" with requests to "move like a snake", or "fly like a falcon." Go over what commands might be given and discuss how these animals move, and why.

A good activity book for grades K–6 is *Project Learning Tree*, by the Western Regional Environmental Education Council and the American Forest Institute, 1319 18th Street N.W., Washington, D.C. 20036.

First Grade. You begin to dig a little deeper with this age group. First graders are curious and they love to figure out puzzles. Who made that track? Who built that nest? Field trip time should not exceed two hours to match this child's attention span. Making maple syrup is a good project because there is an element of magic in it.

Maple syruping is a spring activity of the northern forests. It involves drilling holes 3 inches deep into sugar maple or box elder trees that have a diameter of at least 10 inches. Red or silver maple trees may also be tapped, however the resulting syrup is not as sweet. The hole that is drilled penetrates the outer and inner bark of the tree and stops the upward flow of some of the tree's sap. This sap then flows out of the hole, where it can be collected, boiled down, and used as syrup or sugar.

The Indians would slash the tree, creating a "V" shape, and place a branch that had been cut in half and whittled into a crest shape into the point of the slash. The sap would run out this spile and drip into a birchbark basket. See the book *How Indians Use Wild Plants for Food, Medicine, and Crafts,* by Frances Densmore, Dover Publications, for details on the entire process as done by the Indians.

White culture substituted metal spiles and buckets, and then plastic bags and plastic tubing. The product of any of these collecting methods is gallons of sap which must be heated to boiling and maintained at that point until boiled down into syrup. As long as steam rises from the liquid and water is the prime ingredient, the boiling temperature will be 212 degrees Fahrenheit. When the temperature rises to 219 degrees and the syrup sheets off the spoon, the syrup is ready to eat.

For more information on maple syruping see Scott Nearing's *Maple Sugar Book,* published by Schocken Books. Combine wood cutting, fire building, and tapping the trees, with boiling and tasting the finished product. Combine history with natural history. Read a story while boiling down the sap. Expect a variety of interesting questions. "When do you add the sugar?" "Will it kill the tree to take its sap?" Boil down a very small amount of sap (two gallons) or this activity will take many hours.

Tide pools are exciting places and if your school is located near the ocean this is a good age for looking for variations in life.

Tide pools are located in rock shorelines and are places that hold water even when the tide lowers the rest of the ocean's surface. These are places that are exposed during low tide and become sanctuaries for special forms of life that can live with the surge and withdrawal of the surf.

Sometimes animals are trapped by the withdrawing surf, while other animals are permanent residents of these ocean niches.

Tideline, by Ernest Braun, Viking Press, is an intriguing pictorial look at this kingdom. Students often lose some of their creativity during the school process. Demands for accuracy and peer pressure suppress many exciting and imaginative ideas. The tide pool is a good place to rekindle these ideas. Not all living things have a torso, four appendages, and a head like us. The human body is not the mold for all creation, and a tide pool is the place to expand on that concept.

Second Grade. Two hours with lots of activity is recommended for this age group. Diversity is important in the early years. Specialization is something that can come later.

Insects are more diverse than any other organisms and they are readily available everywhere. They can be raised in a classroom or easily observed in nature.

Sweep nets (butterfly nets) are available from many suppliers. They are easy to use and produce exciting results.

Running through a field of alfalfa or daisies in pursuit of butterflies is as much fun for the teacher as the student. Look at the butterfly, draw it, and color the drawing. It is challenging to mix colors to try matching those in nature. Release the butterfly when you are finished observing it.

Use the sweep net to capture the unseen. Make a few passes through the grass and see how many varieties of insects you catch. Try to imagine how many must be in the entire field.

Place a sheet on the ground beneath a tree and shake the branches. Insects will fall out onto the sheet. How many? How many different kinds? Are they the same as the insects you found in the grass?

Take apart a rotting log and look at the variety of organisms that are in it. Scoop up some soil and sort through it to find organisms. Use magnifying glasses. Take plankton tows in ponds and lakes and use $10-40\times$ power magnification to see the variety of life that can be found in these places.

Third Grade. A half-day experience can be worthwhile with this grade. It is also a good time to begin to give order to their knowledge. Graphing and charting can be done in simple ways.

A vernal pond, a temporary wet area that occurs every spring and dries up every summer, is a good subject for this age because it is a natural system within a small area. Students can measure water temperature and pond depth and keep charts of both.

The students can also observe tracks, birds, frogs, and small mammals, using a plankton net to capture a sample of the life in the pond. This sample can be maintained within the classroom in an aquarium and studied between visits to the vernal pond. In this way the students can compare their aquarium with the pond and look for variations and changes.

Food webs and cycles can be a culmination of this study.

Food webs refer to a relationship between organisms. If you list the plants and animals that are found in an area and then connect the individuals by lines that tie the animal to its food, you will get a web of lines linking animals to animals, and animals to plants. The entire composition will be the food web for the area.

Cycles are the relationships between all factors in a natural area, including the food web. This includes life and death, the movement of water from cloud to land to organism, and many other processes that seem to keep the elements of life continually on the move. Many are simple concepts that can be taught at this level. Mysteries abound. Where do the animals come from? Where do they go when the pond dries up?

Fourth Grade.   Full day field trips should now be introduced. Fourth graders are physically developed enough to learn snowshoeing, cross country skiing, canoeing, outdoor cooking and general camp skills. Their skills in these areas can be improved upon in later grades. The Minnesota Department of Natural Resources has produced a series of study guides on outdoor skills that are appropriate for this grade and older.

Students should continue to learn about the interrelationships that exist in nature. Assign teams of students to observe a single species of bird, reptile, amphibian, or mammal, and to mark on a map all the places that the species goes and what it does. Choose common and easy-to-observe species. On the map you should have an outline of the various plant associations that are in the area, including marsh, hardwoods, stream, conifers, grasslands, crops, lichen, boulder, cactus, or shrub. Does the animal have a wide area of movement? Was the species found in many habitats or is it specialized in its needs? Compare the different kinds of animals and their needs. The same thing can be done with winter tracks.

Eastman Nature Center and the Osseo (Minnesota) School District have developed a nutrition and fitness program for fourth graders. The school and the Center have worked together to develop a two week curriculum which includes a day at the nature center. The program goals are to introduce the students to day hiking and backpacking as a lifetime leisure activity; to demonstrate the importance of nutritional values based on the four basic food groups; to introduce unfamiliar edible foods found along the trail; to be able to recognize the need for an adequate fitness level and to enjoy hiking; to develop skills in outdoor living, such as backpacking, camping, and fire building; and to have the students become aware of individual and group safety.

During the week prior to the field trip, classroom discussions, laboratory sessions, and physical education activities are designed to develop the students' awareness of the outdoors, nutrition, and physical conditioning.

Actual activities undertaken on the field trip include the issuing of scout packs and an explanation of how to adjust and pack them; a half-hour hike with a session on edible foods along the trail and their nutritional value; a workshop on drying fruits; a class session on campsite set-up, camp safety, fire building, and clean-up; and a nature hike with tree and foliage identification. Lunch is prepared by the students themselves.

Fifth Grade.　Add to the skills. Backpacking, snorkeling, studying the compass and map, and improving the fourth grade skills all will expand appreciation of the outdoors. It must be emphasized that actual impact on the environment of all recreation should be minimized.

If the group needs a latrine or a campfire, a trowel should be used to cut the grass mat and to separate the grass sod from the soil beneath it. In this way the sod can be rolled back and saved to cover the area after its use. A fire can be built in this area using just enough wood to accomplish the task. If done properly there will be no charred logs, only ashes, which can be mixed into the soil and then covered by rolling back the piece of sod.

The latrine is done in a similar way by first rolling back the piece

Physical education encompasses more than a gymnasium.
COURTESY PROJECT ADVENTURE, HAMILTON, MASSACHUSETTS.

of sod, and then digging a hole no more than eight inches deep, and piling the soil next to the hole. Each time someone uses the latrine they should put a shovelful of dirt back into the hole. When the latrine is no longer needed, the soil should be smoothed out and the sod replaced. By digging the hole just eight inches deep the nutrients can work for the soil and plants.

Carry out all trash from your campsite, including that which you might find left by some other thoughtless campers. Don't carve the trees, and don't make woodland crafts that will be left behind as evidence of people being in that location. Before you leave an area, do everything you can to make the place look as if no person had ever been there.

Walking Softly in the Wilderness, by John Hart, is an excellent book published by the Sierra Club on this subject, and Laura and Guy Waterman's *Backwoods Ethics,* published by Stonewall Press, is a thought provoking aid to discussion.

Combine skills and studies. Take compass bearings across the landscape and use them as transect lines to gather information.

Sixth Grade. The students are now entering the age of inference and reasoning, and it is a good time to begin to look at human beings as part of the natural cycles. Look at survival from the viewpoint of the individual and the species.

Energy is worth studying at this level. What are natural energy flows? What is consumption, recycling, and waste? How do these terms apply to nature? To the human environment?

Build solar stills and solar collectors. How do wind, sun, and flowing water affect the environment?

Seventh Through Ninth Grade. In many school systems the student is now starting over in new surroundings, with new teachers, new schedules, and new demands. These first years mean tough adjustments. These students are no longer kids, but they are not yet adults. The demand to grow up conflicts with the desire to hang on to the fun of childhood.

This is a time of discipline problems and heartaches for teachers. The environmental education program must offer a challenge and a sense of accomplishment.

Adventurous programs, such as canoe trips, climbing, and advanced survival build good attitudes and personal pride. The study guides offered by the Minnesota Department of Natural Resources are very appropriate at this stage too. Adopt a stream, roadway, or park and keep it clean. Learn what makes it dirty and attack the source. Seek to remedy a problem and achieve a tangible objective.

Physical education can build self-confidence, develop problem-solving capabilities, and bring the student into contact with the outdoors.
COURTESY PROJECT ADVENTURE, HAMILTON, MASSACHUSETTS.

Sometimes a club can be a meaningful extension of student interest. An ecology or outing club can work around many of the classroom scheduling problems.

A set of junior high school activities has been developed in an easy-to-use format called Outdoor Biological Instruction Strategies Packets. These are activities developed by the University of California in Berkeley; information can be obtained by writing to the OBIS Coordinator, Lawrence Hall of Science, University of California, Berkeley, California 94720.

Challenging ideas for a "problem solving" physical education program can be found in the book *Cowstails and Cobras,* published by Project Adventure, P.O. Box 157, Hamilton, MA 01936. This book includes rope courses, initiative games, and other activities which apply physical skills to emotional and mental development.

Tenth Through Twelfth Grade. An expanded social life, sports activities, and job commitments, as well as the standard fifty-minute class scheduling, have made high school outdoor education programs

High school students benefit from outdoor teaching as much as any grade. Don't let the schedule keep them inside.

almost extinct. It will take an innovative teacher to work around these problems, but it has been done and still can be.

Team teaching or the use of substitute teachers may be a way to work out some of the problems. You need a well planned program and presentation, and you will have to sell your ideas to the administration.

Project Learning Tree has an edition for grades seven through twelve which can be incorporated into the educational program during the high school years.

College. This is an age of idealism. It is an experimental time when students are shaking off the last vestiges of parental influence and are seeking to develop new lifestyles. This is a time of evaluation. The college atmosphere encourages students to question, to step back and look at their values and those of society. College life is isolated enough to allow students a life apart from society, yet it tries also to prepare those students for a productive life in society.

Environmental education at best encourages students to question lifestyles and human impact on our physical world. The literature of philosophy and aesthetics is an important part of environ-

College students are branching out, but all their learning should not be confined to a lecture hall.

mental education, as is the study of alternative technologies. But, environmental education must also bridge the gap between college and "real life." Effective action means understanding political issues, physical processes, and the mechanics of public opinion. Outdoor education majors must work with real students and real situations. They cannot afford to limit their experiences to models and role playing.

Foreign Students.   Our universities and high schools welcome many students from other nations. We give these students technical and factual education, and a glimpse of city and campus life, but very little exposure to the natural world. Environmental education is growing in the world context, but very slowly.

America is seen as the grand consumer, the eater of energy and raw materials, overweight in diet and demand—but there is another part of America: the environmental ethic.

The outdoor educator can give the foreign student a glimpse of our wilderness values, an understanding of the American Indian ethic, and a taste for our environmentalist concern. Positive exposure to outdoor activities and values can lead to world-wide concerns about our limited planet and establish a brotherhood beyond political rhetoric.

In the natural world, we are the same species. No other animal speaks our language or looks as we do.

Avoid making comparisons with other places, other experiences, or other memories. Let each object, each moment, and each experience stand by itself before relating it to something else. Look for intrinsic beauty and enjoy each place and moment for all it can give.

Adults. Blend amusement and learning. Adults who attend outdoor educational programs are usually people who already care about the environment and do not want to be preached at. They come to be informed about issues, to improve their skills, and to have a good time. They want to expand their hobbies and they want to be with people who share these interests. The naturalist's attitude is important to their educational experience, the leader must express enthusiasm and excitement. No program can succeed if people do not enjoy being with the leader.

Adults are often reserved in their behavior compared to younger

No one is ever too old to learn.
COURTESY CRAIG R. BORCK.

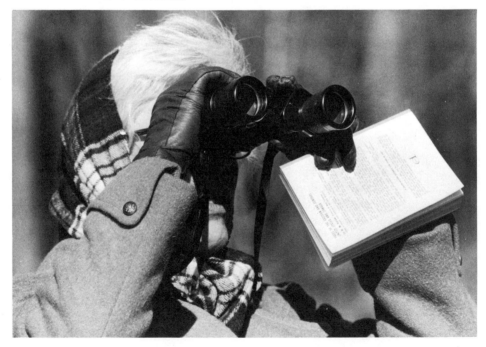

26

groups. Many adults will refuse to try something that might make them look foolish. Consequently, among a group of strangers, questions and comments may be difficult to elicit.

People like to join organizations. Desmond Morris says that it is a desire to achieve a position of leadership that causes people to create organizations. It might be that learning from others increases a person's educational enjoyment and sharing with others increases the sense of achievement. Clubs are a good means of developing an audience. Create programs that suit a club's interests and needs. Serve them while the club serves you.

Mentally Handicapped. Nature is not kind, but neither is it cruel. There is no standard of achievement that all people must reach when they go outdoors. There is no test or goal that is universal. Each person is evaluated by his or her own expectations. What they accomplish will differ with each group and individual, and it is not fair to expect the same result from all students because they are classified as mentally retarded. They have the right to resent doing "baby stuff" just as anyone else would.

The National Easter Seal Society has identified four philosophical concepts for the modern camp program. They state that people with special needs should be given the same experiences that are available to non-handicapped. Camp directors should recognize that special programs can play a major role in the habilitation of people with special needs.

The social recreational values to be derived from association with nature through camping are inherently therapeutic, without regard to any concomitant medical or paramedical benefits that might accrue.

Lastly, group living and working or playing situations provide social and psychological opportunities not available in the clinical or educational settings.

Firsthand sensory experiences are often the most effective types of experiences, since verbalization is often one of the most limiting factors of their learning experiences. Instructions must be simple and clear. It is best to give one instruction and wait until it is carried out before giving another. Including two or three instructions in a single sentence is too confusing. Be careful with your vocabulary.

Simple things that can be observed easily are very successful. Beekeeping and maple syruping are good examples. Bird watching is not too demanding when it is done at a feeder or with a bird bander. A walk can be an exciting event, even without other expectations. Let the mentally handicapped experience things. Don't impose your expectations.

The final consideration for programming with the mentally handicapped is the possibility of integration of mentally handicapped with non-handicapped, particularly in long term resident programs. Dr. Dempsey Hensley, in an article for the American Camping Association, emphasized that there are benefits to integrating a camp.

First there is the humanistic reason: the opportunity for mentally retarded to grow, live, function and learn in a "normal" setting. Secondly, the non-retarded camper learns and grows by adjustment and understanding.

For either of these benefits to accrue there are major considerations for the camp to make. The first is how to select the mentally retarded. The younger the individual, the more accepting he/she may be of difference. The age range of 7–12 is considered highly successful, although all ages can work. The mildly and moderately retarded are the most desirable for this type of program.

The selection process must be based on the person's self-care skills (ability to dress and use the toilet), emotional stability, physical problems, ability to adjust to new situations without family, and play experience with non-retarded in the home environment.

The second concern is whether the program is suited to this type of individual and the staff is adequately prepared. Sometimes good intentions are not enough.

Physically Handicapped. A common mistake of outdoor educators is to offer someone who is handicapped a chance to encounter nature, and then handicap that person further in the guise of protection from everything that *is* nature. Nature has barriers; let the handicapped discover what those barriers are. (See Chapter 10 for further discussion of fear.)

Professor Muir, St. Olaf College, is a sightless botanist who refuses to let lack of vision deter him from teaching botany or canoeing with his wife. To treat him differently, to establish "handicapped" trails for him, would be to destroy his experience.

Not all handicapped people have the same limitations. Let them work to the maximum of their abilities and senses.

In 1978 Professor John Kennedy of Toronto's Scarborough College concluded seven years of research on blind perception. In his presentation he told the American Psychological Association:

> They [blind people] can draw; they can recognize; they can use elements like lines and dots; they can understand whole shapes or parts; they can select what is important and capture that; they can

recognize ambiguities; they can appreciate how two drawings will be more specific about an object than one.

Their drawings showed motion by using bent limbs and adding small circles to suggest movement, and they made wheels show movement by curving the spokes, adding overlapping circles and placing a wheel on a hill and drawing wheels along a path of movement.

In pointing to the corners of a room, they make their pointing arms converge more and more as they walk away from the corners.

The inevitable conclusion is that the principles that underlie line representation belong to a perceptual system that is not restricted to vision. It is a system of principles that is common to haptics (sense of touch) and to vision.

As we learn more we may find out that the only thing holding back the handicapped is the non-handicapped.

The Sierra Club's Inner City Outings program works with urban youth and special needs groups. The Environmental Traveling Companions of San Francisco sponsor backpacking, skiing and river raft trips for the disabled. Camp Allen, in Bedford, New Hampshire, Outward Bound and Camp Courage in Minnesota, and Berkeley Outreach Recreation Program, Inc., are some other organizations that are working with state and federal agencies to give the handicapped a better wilderness experience.

Outward Bound's policy statement for working with the handicapped states:

We believe that when the able bodied and the physically disabled share in stress and adversity, three things happen. First, it becomes clear that every person has a disability—it is just that some are more obvious than others. Second, it demonstrates that a disability is frequently not as limiting as a person assumes it is. And third, both the able bodied and the disabled recognize that they have more in common with each other when emphasis is placed on abilities rather than disabilities. The question, then, is not whether you can or cannot do it, but whether you are willing to try.

In an article in *Sierra* magazine, writer Kerry Drager states, "The trails enjoyed most by visually impaired people are those left in as natural a state as possible; if a trail is interesting to all the senses of a sighted person, it will be interesting to the blind."

A little foresight in trail planning will avoid obvious hazard areas and open most trails to people of varying physical abilities. Perhaps some insight will eliminate the ugly railings that clutter some beautiful cliffs to protect "non-handicapped" from falling off. If trails are designed to minimize impact on the land and to eliminate overt dangers, the variety of landscapes will allow able bodied and disabled people to choose those best suited to their own needs.

Delinquents. There is a growing philosophy that the outdoors provides an appropriate place for value clarification and development of self esteem, while isolating the delinquent from the stimuli of the home. This has led to many camp–school programs which combine schooling with adventure.

The expectations of the outdoor education teacher must reflect this reality; these students have not chosen to be there because they enjoy the outdoors; they are required to be there by the law. They are in a program for behavior modification. The outdoors is a tool, but it is not the main purpose of the program. The outdoor program works because it substitutes the excitement of the outdoors for street danger and provides a reason for cooperation and teamwork.

Once these conditions are understood, the outdoor educator should then work within that framework to infuse environmental ethics and values into the course. A program that does not reflect those factors is delinquent in its institutional behavior.

The Fund for Advancement of Camping has become involved in "Youth-at-Risk" programming and has agreed to establish a clearing house which would develop a directory of available programs, develop dialogue between the organizations and institutions involved in the programs, provide a basis for standards and policies, and aid in research related to working with and for the youth in need of rehabilitative services.

This involvement is based on the fact that 1.5 million youths appear in juvenile court each year and 4.5 million are involved with the police each year.

Kendall Lingle, in an article for The American Camping Association magazine *Camping*, lists ten types of alternative programs that are in operation at the present time.

1. Long-term therapeutic camps
2. Stress/adventure programs
3. Public school programs
4. Juvenile court alternatives
5. Civilian Conservation Corp/Youth Conservation Corp forestry camps
6. Independent organizations

7.   Resident therapeutic schools
8.   Shelter residences
9.   Government corrections institutes
10. Resident private school programs

Lingle points out that there are no common guidelines or common authority. Members belong to The Association for Experiential Education, The American Camping Association, or The American Correctional Association, respectively, but no membership in a national organization is required.

In analyzing the programs Lingle found that they all have certain program goals in common: they all stress a work ethic; work to re-establish respect for adults; try to develop self esteem; and teach students to place emphasis on success, not failure, recognize need for rules of conduct, respect other's strengths and limits, and think objectively.

Religious Groups. Church groups have developed bad reputations in some areas because their activities are too social and do not reflect the reverence for the land that many users of a wilderness area have.

Nature should be a part of the religious experience as it has been for John Burroughs, Sigurd Olson, John Muir, and Ralph Waldo Emerson. The church should be the biggest environmental force in the world.

In 1980 the Sigurd Olson Institute in Ashland, Wisconsin, initiated a conference on the church and nature. The conference's intent is for this dialogue to re-establish or reaffirm the church's concern for nature. For more information on this program, contact The Sigurd Olson Institute, Northland College, Ashland, Wisconsin 54806.

> There seems to me a fundamental distinction between God the Creator and God the Ruler. God the Creator is the God of mystery, a presence felt but not known. God the Ruler is a man-god, limited by (and to) the human understanding. God the Creator rules by creating, by the continuous ramification and metamorphosis of formal energy, as the life forms keep rising out of and falling back into the earth. But God the Ruler rules by decree and by whim, like a tyrant, like the tyrants who invented him. If God rules as Creator, then worship involves the humility of creating, aligning oneself with the creation and drawing on its energy, not the mindless and inert humility of obedience to "revealed" laws.
>
> WENDELL BERRY, *A Continuous Harmony,*
> Harcourt Brace Jovanovich

Three

What to Expect

I went to the woods because I wished to live deliberately, to front only the essential facts of life, and see if I could not learn what it had to teach, and not, when I came to die, discover that I had not lived.

HENRY DAVID THOREAU

No one can predict the final effectiveness of an outdoor approach to teaching. The only thing that is certain is that you will have added one more method to your teaching repertoire and the students will have encountered more stimuli than students in classes that do not go outside.

The need for the outdoor classroom is stated in the National Education Association's resolution in 1973:

The National Education Association believes the nation's priorities must include the protection of our environment. It urges the development and improvement of federal legislation, programs, and appropriations that provide education: (a) for use, stewardship, and preservation of a viable environment; (b) to eliminate pollution; (c) to promote an understanding by students and the public of the effects of past, present, and future population growth patterns on world civilization and human survival; and (d) to promote establishment of federal Wilderness Areas.

The Association urges its affiliates to support environmental programs in school systems for grades K through adult.

The Association encourages local affiliates to establish procedures to assure that policies and practices adopted by governing boards are consistent with environmental concerns.

To meet this need, the outdoor-oriented program must be as well thought-out as the indoor counterpart. Lesson plans may be more open-ended because of an unpredictability and the variables involved, but there must be an understood set of goals for the overall program.

The state of Iowa set the following goals for its environmental education program:

1. To develop an awareness of the components of the physical, biological, and cultural environment and how the pieces fit together.
2. To develop an appreciation of the needs of society for natural resources and limitations of those resources.
3. To develop a working knowledge of the fundamentals of the sciences and their application to natural resource management and consumption.
4. To clarify value systems regarding humanity's responsibility to our present and future environment.
5. To develop an understanding of the political and economic interactions involved in deciding between alternatives.

The UNESCO Environmental Education Workshop in Belgrade offered these as international goals:

1. To improve the relationship of humanity with nature and human beings to each other: a) For each nation, according to its culture, to clarify for itself the meaning of such basic concepts as "quality of life" and "human happiness" in the context of the total environment, with an extension of the clarification and appreciation to cultures beyond one's national boundaries. b) To identify which actions will ensure the preservation and improvement of humanity's potentials and develop social and individual well-being in harmony with the biophysical and artificial environments.
2. To develop a world population which is *aware* of, and *concerned* about, the environment and its associated problems, and which has the *knowledge, skills, attitudes, motivations,*

UNESCO's goals include the clarification of quality of life and human happiness in the environment.

and *commitment* to work individually and collectively toward solutions to current problems, and the prevention of new ones.

To work towards these major goals, the following objectives were set:

Iowa

1. The student will develop an awareness, an appreciation, and a concern for the immediate environment.
2. The student will learn about the various components that comprise the natural and artificial environment.
3. The student will gain knowledge about the basic environmental concepts that affect life including the conservation of natural resources.
4. The student will be able to think critically and make value judgments about humanity's impact on the environment and the societal and environmental changes resulting from natural resource use.
5. The student will understand the public policy decision-making process and be able to make inputs into current environmental decisions.

1. Awareness: To help individuals and social groups acquire strong feelings of concern for the environment and the motivation for actively participating in its protection and improvement.
2. Knowledge: To help individuals and social groups acquire basic understanding of the total environment, its associated problems and humanity's critically responsible presence and role in it.
3. Attitude: To help individuals and social groups acquire social values and the ability to make sound choices while developing in them a sensitivity to the environment.
4. Skills: To help individuals and social groups acquire the skills for solving environment problems.
5. Evaluation Ability: To help individuals and social groups evaluate environmental measures and education programs in terms of ecological, political, economic, social and educational factors.
6. Participation: To help individuals and social groups move toward taking the necessary action to resolve environmental problems.

The Belgrade conference further defined the principles that should guide an environmental education program (EE):

1. EE should consider the environment in its totality—natural and artificial, ecological, political, economic, technological, social, cultural and aesthetic.
2. EE should be a continuous life-long process, both in school and out of school.
3. EE should be interdisciplinary in its approach.
4. EE should emphasize active participation in preventing and solving environmental problems.
5. EE should examine major environmental issues from a world point of view while paying due regard to regional differences.
6. EE should focus on current and future environmental situations.
7. EE should examine all development and growth from an environmental perspective.

8. EE should promote the value of local, national and international cooperation in the solution of environmental problems.

In Minnesota a committee of environmental educators worked with an environmental education specialist from the Minnesota Department of Education to try to define the environmental education process even further. They named five different levels of an environmental education program.

Level one is the *Activity Level* which receives input from many curriculum distributors and involves the "what-to-do" stage of teaching. Many of the following chapters will provide you with activities.

Level two involves *Learner Outcomes* (expectations of results). This step had not been catalogued successfully in the literature that was available to the committee and, therefore, the committee's task was to try to define these outcomes.

The third level defines the *Concepts* that lead to the individual goals. Concepts become the building blocks of understanding and the foundation of environmental education.

A concept is a lumping of facts and theories into an understanding of a principle. A concept is more intangible than a fact. It is an extension of ideas and knowledge toward understanding complexity.

There are some people who never rise beyond the naming of things, which is not knowledge, merely memorization. That is not to say that facts are not important. Classification is an indispensable tool, as are readily available facts that are relevant to a profession or skill, but facts are just the first step in learning.

Weller Embler in the quarterly journal *ETC.: A Review of General Semantics* wrote, "If knowledge of naming and of facts, if the accumulation of information and the testing and weighing of it are the materials of learning, creative use of the materials, as in the making of judgments and the finding of truths is the final goal of learning—that is, of an education."

Goals is the fourth level of an environmental education program. In order to identify educational goals, the group found it necessary to determine the context under which the goals would be taught. The following four contexts represent their chosen spectrum of environmental experiences.

1. Natural Context: That learning which is most related to non-human-dominated communities and their physical habitats, for example, soils, atmospheric and hydrologic systems, animals, plants, the distribution and abundance of organisms, decomposers and decomposition processes, nutrient and mineral cycles, and energy systems.

2. Social Context: That learning which is most related to social, economic, political, cultural, ethical, and psychological systems.
3. Valuing Context: That learning which is most related to choosing freely from a thoughtful consideration of alternatives, becoming aware of what we cherish and affirming these choices by connecting them to our own overt behavior. Values clarification questions are "you" questions. What does it mean to *you?* What difference has this made in *your* life? What did *you* learn that was important to *you?* How do *you* live differently as a result of what *you* have learned?
4. Action Context: That learning which is most related to the identification, evaluation, and testing of alternatives to community environmental problems; the political and social communication skills required in their resolution, and service to the community.

The fifth level, the culmination of all others, is *Philosophy,* which is the rich personal experience of establishing values based on fact and experience.

MINNESOTA ENVIRONMENTAL LEARNER OUTCOMES

I. Learners should be able to understand ecological systems

A. Concepts

1. population
2. environment
3. ecosystem
4. community
5. life cycle
6. individual
7. habitat
8. food chains/webs
9. interdependency
10. producer
11. consumer
12. decomposer
13. chemical cycling
14. cycles
15. limiting factor
16. interaction, e.g., competition, predation, parasitism, etc.
17. carrying capacity
18. succession
19. niche

B. Learner Outcomes

1. General

a. Describe an interdependency that occurs in the environment.
b. Describe an environmental change and give a consequence.
c. Describe humans as an integral part of the natural world, influenced by natural processes.

2. Elementary
    a. Understand the basic concept of an ecosystem.
    b. Demonstrate knowledge of the components of an ecosystem.
    c. Demonstrate knowledge of the physical factors of an ecosystem.
    d. Demonstrate knowledge of the roles of producers, consumers, and decomposers in ecosystems.
    e. Demonstrate knowledge of simple cycles in ecosystems, such as the water cycle.

3. Secondary
    a. Describe a relationship between an ecological and sociological or political system.
    b. Give an example of the dynamic balance of nature.
    c. Identify a living organism characteristic of a particular ecosystem. Describe why it is found there.
    d. Trace the flow of energy through an ecosystem.
    e. Describe factors that result in ecosystem persistence.

II. Learners should be provided with experiences which will assist in the development of personal appreciation, sensitivity, and stewardship for the environment.
    A. Concepts
1.	belief systems	11.	culture
2.	cooperation	12.	values
3.	aesthetics	13.	landscape patterns
4.	reverence	14.	symbolism
5.	love	15.	design
6.	morals	16.	appetite
7.	stewardship	17.	beauty
8.	benevolence	18.	conflict
9.	recreation	19.	happiness
10.	ethics		

    B. Environmental Learner Outcomes
        1. General
            a. Relate whether the student feels a personal commitment to the environment.
            b. Describe some cultural differences and their influence on the environment.

2. Elementary

   a. Recognize the effects of diversity in nature.

   b. Work cooperatively in teams toward the accomplishment of a goal.

   c. Relate the student's personal perceptions of an environmental place or event.

   d. Develop outdoor recreational skills.

3. Secondary

   a. Understand some of the relationships between belief system literature and the environmental values of various cultures.

   b. Distinguish appetite (I like), knowledge (I know), ethics (I judge), and morals (I act).

   c. Demonstrate knowledge of the influence of the mass media on shaping our perception of an aesthetic environment.

   d. Evaluate an argument where socioeconomic interests are contrasted with aesthetic considerations.

III. Learners should be able to understand cause-and-effect relationships between humans and the environment.

  A. Concepts

1.	energy production and utilization	10.	habitat management
2.	food production	11.	threats and hazards
3.	waste	12.	appropriate technology
4.	building construction	13.	steady state
5.	eugenics	14.	technology fix
6.	weather manipulation	15.	recreation
7.	resource use	16.	cause-and-effect
8.	pollutants	17.	multiple use
9.	pesticides, herbicides, and fertilizers	18.	renewable
		19.	nonrenewable

  B. Environmental Learner Outcomes

    1. General

      a. Organize, analyze, synthesize, and interpret information from varied sources.

      b. Describe resource management practices for terrestrial and aquatic ecosystems.

        c. Describe how student's own personal beliefs and values influence use of resources.

        d. Describe and analyze environmental threats and hazards after weighing the evidence and considering all the available information.

        e. Demonstrate knowledge of the impact of agriculture and technology on two ecosystems: terrestrial and aquatic.

        f. Demonstrate knowledge that habitat management is an effective technique of wildlife arrangement to either maintain or increase the numbers of animal populations.

2. Elementary

        a. Assess human impact on the environment, listing causes and effects.

        b. Demonstrate knowledge that water is a reusable resource and that as our use of water increases it is necessary to establish water use policies.

        c. Define pollutants and describe the effects of increased levels of pollutants on the environment.

3. Secondary

        a. Describe and evaluate alternatives to the management of the earth's finite natural resources which most effectively perpetuate them.

        b. Use political processes to gain support for positions.

        c. Describe a steady state human social system in harmony with the environment, and explain the consequences of such a system.

IV. Learners should be able to understand the decision-making processes of individuals and institutions.

  A. Concepts

1. economics	10.	laws
2. politics	11.	power, e.g., institutional/
3. belief systems		individual
4. peer pressure	12.	compromise
5. customs	13.	technology assessment
6. education	14.	health
7. technology	15.	rights
8. communication	16.	National Environmental
9. organizations		Policies

B. Environmental Learner Outcomes
   1. General
      a. Describe the roles of citizens in policy formation.
      b. Explain and evaluate an environmental issue in student's community.
   2. Elementary
      a. Give examples of personal impact on the environment and suggest ways to reduce it.
      b. Identify the central issue in an environmental dispute.
      c. Demonstrate knowledge of some effects of technology on the environment.
      d. Suggest some constructive ways of resolving an environmental conflict.
   3. Secondary
      a. Give examples of the influences of beliefs and values on environmental decisions (for example, family, peer, school, community, nation and world).
      b. Demonstrate knowledge of an environmental issue where political, educational, economic, and governmental institutions play a role.
      c. Describe the influence of technology and communications on individual and institutional decision-making.
      d. Identify some of the relationships between political and economic power and environmental decisions.

V. Learners should be able to evaluate alternative responses to environmental concerns or issues before deciding on a course of action or no action.
   A. Concepts
      1. facts
      2. opinions
      3. inferences
      4. assumptions
      5. decision-making processes
      6. values and attitudes
      7. problem-solving approaches
      8. beliefs
      9. indicators
      10. family planning
   B. Environmental Learner Outcomes
      1. General
         a. Describe how personal values and attitude affect behavior.

      b. Compare alternative modes of action for solving a problem, and select and defend a position.

      c. Describe and explain own feelings and beliefs regarding a particular issue, such as the question of hunting, and select and defend a position.

  2. Elementary

      a. Distinguish between statements of fact and opinion.

      b. Choose or not choose to participate in environmental activities in the home, school, or community, and give reasons for choice.

  3. Secondary

      a. Describe an objective decision-making process and contrast it with a subjective decision-making process.

      b. Describe students' rational responses and emotional responses about a community, state, national, and international environmental dilemma, and explain the basis for each choice.

VI. Learners should be able to understand ways in which planning/nonplanning influences the future.

  A. Concepts

1. economics	11. alternative futures
2. human welfare	12. extrapolation
3. population	13. forecasting
4. energy	14. assessment
5. lifestyle	15. divergent thinking
6. resources	16. images
7. education	17. paradigm, for example,
8. belief systems	theoretical model
9. consumerism	18. scenario
10. global consciousness	

  B. Environmental Learner Outcomes

    1. General

      a. Describe a short-term and long-term effect of an action on human social systems.

      b. Contrast the advantages and disadvantages of a short-term and long-term solution to an environmental dilemma.

      c. Describe ways in which environmental problems are caused by unforeseen consequences of human actions.

2. Elementary
   a. Describe one short-term and one long-term effect of an action on any ecosystem.
   b. Identify at least two alternatives for dealing with an environmental dilemma, explain the consequences of each alternative, and select and defend a position.
3. Secondary
   a. Demonstrate a futures approach in problem solving (for example, the use of a futures wheel, cross impact matrix, relevance tree).
   b. Make a trend extrapolation based on data from tables and graphs, and identify assumptions.

Try to mix contexts and subject matter. Environmental education encompasses all disciplines. We live in a closed system and each action affects and is affected by all others. Environmental education is the act of stepping back and recognizing our own place in the world.

Four

Activities
for Class
and Community

One's own landscape comes in time to be a sort of outlying part of
himself; he has sowed himself broadcast upon it, and it reflects his
own moods and feelings; he is sensitive to the verge of the horizon;
cut those trees and he bleeds; mar those hills, and he suffers.

JOHN BURROUGHS

Outdoor education doesn't mean moving from one building into
another, even if the other building is a nature center. Use class time to
make your outdoor time more effective, but get out as soon as you can.

The transition from indoors to outdoors is difficult for many
teachers and students. All new situations demand an extra effort on
the part of the whole group. The first outing may establish only that
learning extends beyond the building and that discipline can be
maintained outside the classroom. The goal of a first outing might be
to establish a comfortable feeling for the outdoors. You must strive to
create an atmosphere in which the students can learn through experience. An initial positive experience will set the tone for future field
trips and improve results.

All facts and stimuli are going to register and relate to previously
known and understood information. We cannot expect students from
inner cities, who have had only minimal exposure to forests through
the media, to feel good about the lacy network of green that is between

them and the sun unless there is sufficient time to interact with the area, develop an enjoyable relationship, and explore.

An hour and a half session at a nature center that your class visits once each year is not going to break down the fears that have developed over a lifetime. It is only one step in a process of in-class and out-of-class exposures to nature. Fears take time to disintegrate.

Creating a comfortable learning atmosphere depends on your own interests and personality. The best method is to make the transition naturally. Use normal assignments with an outdoor slant. Assign stories in reading that have a natural history basis. Calculate board feet in math, study local topographic maps in geography. Cook wild foods in home economics, make bird feeders in industrial arts. Use music class to explore natural sounds. Look at paintings and photos of wild areas in art. Use films, filmstrips, slides and all the normal teaching accessories. Just look for a nature angle.

Invite nature to be a part of the indoors through plants and animals. A terrarium is a miniature world in which you can control the weather and select the plants you wish. It is a microcosm of the natural world and can be both a prelude and follow-up to a field trip. However, terrarium building can be overdone and it is better to let things grow in the woods rather than inside of a classroom. Make group terrariums rather than individual ones.

We depend on the plant world fully as much as the wild animals do.

Terrarium possibilities include habitat studies. Each group could make a representative habitat grouping (for example, marsh, woods, meadow, desert). Study the different needs of various plants, such as types of soils, amounts of water and sunlight, as you build. Then try making some terrariums from seeds that you have collected yourself.

Aquatic terrariums can easily turn to aquariums, and terrestrial terrariums can be worked into vivariums for reptiles and amphibians and insect habitats.

If the terrarium is properly built, maintenance is almost completely unnecessary. Moisture will condense on the sides and rain back down, creating a self-sustaining unit.

STEPS FOR PLANTING A TERRARIUM

1. Line the container with moss, green side out, and chips of charcoal.
2. Spread gravel over the bottom.
3. Add a layer of sand and charcoal.
4. Humus or topsoil layer.
5. Plant large background first and then the rest of the plants.
6. Cover the roots with soil and moss and bits of charcoal.
7. Water and cover.
8. Start in sunless place for one week and then move into the sun.
9. Watch for condensation on the glass to determine water quantity. Leave open to remove some moisture if necessary.

What You Will Need

1. Moss
2. Gravel
3. Charcoal
4. Plants
5. Natural inanimate objects
6. Spoon
7. Scissors
8. Tongs
9. Straight dowel to aid planting in a narrow-necked bottle

Table 4.1 tells how much soil and gravel is needed for different sized terrariums.

Table 4.1.   Ratios of Soil and Gravel to Terrarium Size

Bottle Height	Inches of Soil	Inches of Gravel
5 inches	1¼	3/16
10 inches	2½	5/16
12 inches	3	3/8
24 inches	6	3/4

Questions for Study and Discussion

1. Are the plants being collected from sunny or shady places?
2. Is the area damp, soggy, or dry?
3. Discuss water, carbon and nitrogen cycles of plants.
4. What is humus?
5. Why do we want gravel and charcoal in the terrariums?

Project.   Make a terrarium container using pre-cut glass. You will need:

2 pieces—10″ × 8″ (sides)
2 pieces—10″ × 16″ (top and bottom)
2 pieces—16″ × 8″ (sides)

Apply sealant to the inside seams, tape the corners, and shellac the tape. If desired, set in plaster of paris for a sturdier base or build on a wooden base that can be picked up and moved to different locations. The glass should not be lifted. Prepare the terrarium by layering clean gravel or a broken flower pot, 1 inch of sand and charcoal, 2 inches of garden soil, and a layer of leaf mold or moss. Plant the terrarium to represent a certain habitat.

Take the temperature and humidity readings of the terrarium and compare with the temperature and humidity readings of the actual habitat. What adjustments are necessary?

Remember:

1. Do not overcrowd.
2. Cover bare patches with moss.
3. Add rocks, acorns, or other natural items for interest.

4. Make a pond by burying a container in the soil and rim it with moss and stones.

5. Do not use grass because it will grow too fast and too tall.

6. Clean the sides of the terrarium with a detergent containing ammonia. If you clean the inside, do not use ammonia when the plants are in. After the terrarium habitat has been established, use a clean rag for wiping the glass.

STEPS FOR MAKING A NATIVE FISH AQUARIUM

1. Set up empty aquariums with clean gravel, plants, snails, and water from the lake or stream. Let it sit for one or two days.

2. Aerate the tank well. The stream and lake fish are more used to cool water than tropical fish and an aerator helps. This will also prevent some fungus growth.

3. Place the tank in the shade.

4. Do not overcrowd.

5. Add two teaspoons of rock salt per gallon of water the first day and one additional teaspoon per gallon on the second. This helps prevent disease. *Never add more.* Salt will not evaporate, so you will not have less than what you started with.

6. Be selective in what you take.

    a. Minnows (shiners, dace, fatheads) are excellent and will eat all fish foods.

    b. Bullheads are hardy and will keep the tank clean. The yellow cat, which is often called a bullhead, is not a good cleaner, since it depends on a meat diet and will eat only live critters.

    c. Sunfish are colorful and fun, but they are territorial and may be hard on the other small fish. With other sunnies of the same size they will often settle for a territory out of necessity. It is better to have four or five sunfish than just two.

    d. Darters are found in the clear lakes on sandy or rocky bottoms and are attractive fish. However, they require live food or frozen daphnia or brine shrimp.

7. Do not allow the tank to get rancid from detritus. Overfeeding will cause the excess to settle on the bottom and around rocks and will kill the fish as a result of fish rot and the gases it produces.

The act of going out for a short time, bringing life back inside, and sustaining that life is important. Going out for a short period with a purpose leads to longer, less structured outings. The student should take only those things which are abundant and can be sustained in the classroom, and no more than the amount needed. This establishes an understanding of ethics and basic ecology.

The more often students go outdoors, the more they will learn about the outdoor environment. Just sitting under a tree on the school lawn to draw, write, or read helps establish the outdoor classroom.

Students' learning can be increased by extra assignments. Ask students to compose a bird list for the class each month, listing the birds that are observed while riding the bus or walking to school.

Ask students to observe and report weather conditions and weather signs. Select one student each day to predict the weather for the coming day, with the aid of the classroom barometer.

One of the favorite projects of a Minnesota naturalist and outdoor educator is the collection of monarch butterflies, which he tags and releases as part of a study with the University of Toronto. He nets the butterflies, records the sex, condition, and where found, removes some scales, and puts on gummed tags to mark the individual. One of his tagged butterflies was recovered in Mexico.

He also rears some monarch caterpillars in captivity, which allows students to observe the metamorphic process. He then tags the butterflies and releases them. In some school programs the culmination of the in-class session is the tagging and releasing of the insects in the schoolyard.

Not all animals make good classroom specimens and you must demonstrate an ethical understanding of animal needs and populations when choosing what you will work with. Do not take an animal that needs great range and try to confine it to a cage.

Establish an animal hospital in your classroom. Veterinarians do not have the time to work with broken winged songbirds or nestlings that have been abandoned because their nest has fallen out of a tree. There are always injured animals wherever machines are found. The success that you might enjoy in helping an injured animal will teach ecology, ethics, and responsibility.

Often a member of a local Audubon Chapter who has cared for many injured animals will help you get started. A Guide to the Care of Injured Wildlife by the National Audubon Society, Western Regional Office, and Small Wild Orphans, by the Animal Humane Society, are good booklets to use.

Many animals are protected by law to prevent people from taking wildlife as pets. This protects wild animals that require more care and understanding than most people realize, and it probably prevents people from unwanted bites and scratches from scared or untamable animals. A permit from the state natural resources department and the Federal Fish and Wildlife Service is required to take care of some injured animals and many animals will have to be turned over to other parties, such as local universities, for continued treatment. Even the act of getting animals to proper treatment facilities will be a learning experience.

You might investigate the values that are associated with house plants and pets and some of the consequences of those values. An activity that looks at our own life in relation to the natural world is a good bridge to a field trip into that natural world.

The history of a region begins with its geology and meteorology, for the shaping of the Earth determined where the plants would be found. The flora determined the fauna and the resource mix determined where mankind went. A good understanding of this history will create a greater impact in your teaching.

State historical societies, old books, old pictures, historic sites, senior citizens, and local historical societies, can help piece together human history. Use these assets and resources with imagination. Borrow old pictures from the local community and use them for the basis of a booklet or a comic book. You might lay them out as a story, take photocopies, and then write in comic book captions. Use your local newspaper as a reference. Back issues can be a treasure chest of inspiration. Libraries often have special collections on an area's history; your librarian can help you locate the information you need.

Our communities offer many opportunities for study, and the following exercises can be used for a sequential class program or individual studies.

INTRODUCTORY ACTIVITY: WHAT IS A COMMUNITY?

A community is a geographical location which provides the basic necessities of life to its inhabitants. These basic needs are water, air, shelter, food, and space to live in. We often break the concept of a community into two arbitrary divisions: natural communities and human communities.

A natural community under this definition would provide habitats for organisms other than man. We can list some natural communities such as forest, fields, and aquatic systems. Each of these can be broken down into smaller categories. For example, aquatic systems include bogs, marshes, lakes, ponds, streams, and oceans. However, for the present, we can be content to use these larger categories and generalize about their characteristics. Each one has a specific combination of temperature, water, soil and sunlight, and these conditions create a favorable environment for certain plant populations. The plant food, in combination with the environmental factors, then determines the animal varieties. The community can be thought of as a life support system with each community's components varying slightly.

Within the community many interactions exist between individuals. Animals are mobile and may move between plant communities to obtain their needs.

The dictionary defines a community as "a society of people living in proximity to each other, in one locality, under the same conditions of life, and having some common bonds or organization, political or religious, which makes them a more or less closely knit unit." This definition is for the human category, but it seems inadequate unless the basic habitat requirements are provided. Humans are more mobile than many other animals and they also move between communities for their needs.

In many ways there are similarities between these two community types and we can learn about one by studying the other.

Activity

The Natural Community. All students choose an animal that they like or are interested in. No one should know what the other students choose. Each student should describe animal's needs in as much detail as possible. This activity may also be used as a Twenty-Questions game in which students try to determine each other's animal by questions about its habitat.

Without disclosing the species identification, students should describe their animal by its needs. Group the animals according to similar needs to form community groups. Then identify the animals and see if, in fact, they do share the same areas.

The Human Community. Have students analyze another animal:—themselves. Each student should complete the "Personal Analysis" sheet.

Group the children by temperature preference first. Then group them by their area preference. If there is a great difference in food choices, divide the students again. These are their communities.

The temperatures will always be what they listed. The woods are just woods, they do not include lakes or streams. Lakes have non-wooded shorelines. Food preferences are combined and make up the only foods available to the group. Do these foods need different

Caring for an injured animal is one way of learning about its needs.

conditions to live in then those they have chosen? If so, they must be imported.

Can they perform their favorite activities in this community as it is now described, or would they have to go somewhere else for some activities? Too warm a temperature would eliminate winter activities, living in the woods will not provide a place for ocean swimming, and living in a city will not give them a place to hunt.

Each community group of students should now meet to plan their community. List what they want in it, and how each would interact with the items they describe.

Discuss differences and similarities between the natural and human communities that they have described. How much did they have to alter their community?

COMMUNITY INTERACTIONS

In all communities there are many interactions. We may interact directly with an object by consuming it. Indirectly we interact with the components that were consumed or created by the product of our consumption. All communities have associations (expected partnerships). An example of an association between plants might be red and jack pines. They do not need each other, but can be found growing near one another so often that we expect to see one with the other. They share many of the same habitat requirements.

Our relationships with other objects may be spatial (walk around it), physical (ride it), intellectual (communication), or neutral (sharing our habitat without establishing any type of contact with us).

Many of our relationships may be explained in terms of symbiosis, which can be defined as living together. In the plants called lichens we find an alga and a fungi living in such close relationship that they appear as one plant, totally different from the original components. Because both plants benefit, we call this mutualism.

Another form of mutualism is the relationship between the termite and the protozoa that lives in its gut. The termite can bite the wood, but cannot digest the cellulose without the aid of the protozoa.

When one object receives benefit from the other without harm or benefit for the second party, this is called commensalism. The relationship of the remora that attaches itself to the shark and then cleans up the scraps after dinner is one example. If one of the objects gains benefit at the expense of another, it is called parasitism.

Humans are also subject to the natural cycles: carbon, nitrogen, water, phosphorus and oxygen. We can be predators or prey, and we can decompose and provide nutrient for other life.

In the following activities we will explore these complexities in our community.

Activity

1. Fill out an interrelationship list to analyze man's interactions. Begin with three items suggested by the instructor and then have the students add any five items from their community. All indirect items should be from the natural community. For example:

Item	*Association*	*Direct Dependency*	*Indirect Dependency*
shoe	sock	leather	grass to feed cow
chair	table	wood	squirrel plants seed

2. Symbiotic relationships exist between humans and pets, in relationships between people of different status, and people functioning in the urban or natural world. Fill out a sheet of symbiotic relationships based on your community. For example:

Mutualism	*Parasitism*	*Commensalism*
pet dog	extortion	man feeds cattle
songwriter/musician	plagerism	fish hatcheries

3.   Each of us functions in a variety of complex cycles. Make a food web, see chapter 2, using your two favorite foods. After completing your food web, make one for each of the following cycles and include yourself in the cycle.

Carbon   Oxygen   Water   Nitrogen

4.   The Earth has often been described as a spaceship hurtling through space with all of the systems to support life on board. If anything goes wrong with those systems, the passengers will be in danger. Now suppose you are blasting into space on an even smaller spacecraft and you are allowed only ten different items to take along for your survival. What would you take? You may never return to Earth, so be prepared to survive somewhere else. All the craft has is a shell, seats, and all the mechanical apparatus to make it fly. Size is not a problem. List the 10 items you would take and explain why.

COMMUNITY INTERACTIONS AND CHANGE

We define our natural communities according to their environmental factors and plant associations. Occasionally we become so short-sighted that we view them as fixed blocks of real estate that will remain the same until man decides to alter them. However, each plant community we view is in transition and every natural community is undergoing change. This progressive change is called succession. Human communities also go through a series of changes from village to metropolis.

We also view our communities as immobile entities, but the waters flow from one community to another, the woods' edge progresses into the field, and the marsh envelops and then covers the pond. Animals move from one community to another to fulfill their own needs.

Neighboring communities provide some goods to sustain the mobile inhabitants of another community. In the same way, human communities exchange goods. A major difference between natural and human community exchange is that we have the ability to bring our needs to where we are, rather than individually going out after our needs.

Activity

1.   Describe reasons for a woods to take over a meadow. Describe reasons for and means by which a human population would take over another region.

2. In addition to interactions between static populations of different communities, we also have transient populations which float between communities. These are variable sources of energy and conflict within a community, and include such things as migrating populations of birds, mammals, insects, and tourist populations or people who adjust to weather by traveling to locations which provide the proper climate.

Take your Personal Analysis sheet and plot the places you would have to be each month to maintain your favorite temperature range. Make your home area part of the sequence of places for the time of year when its weather conforms to your choice.

3. How has transportation influenced your community? Assign ages to segments of your community. Where were the first stores and

```
PERSONAL ANALYSIS SHEET

The temperatures I enjoy most are:

   -50 -  0 F ___
     0 - 32   ___
    32 - 50   ___
    50 - 70   ___
    70 - 80   ___
    over 80   ___


My favorite activities are:

    1. _____
    2. _____
    3. _____
    4. _____


My favorite foods are (Be Very Specific):

    1. _____
    2. _____


I like the following area best:

    the city   ___          lake    ___
    country    ___          river   ___
    woods      ___          ocean   ___
    desert     ___          prairie ___
    mountains  ___
```

major development? Did your town grow in increments? How has transportation changed in your community and what is its effect? Many towns can show a change from river travel to coach to train to highway to freeway by the age distribution of its buildings or building sites. What other factors have influenced your community's growth?

4.   Do any wild animals visit your human community to fulfill their needs? Why? (Example: bird feeders)

5.   Population changes are responses to many conditions. The Sigurd Olson Institute in Ashland, Wisconsin, did a study on the movement of people to the North Country of Wisconsin. Initially they plotted the population as given in the census for each decade since 1900. This indicated the long term growth rate. In this instance, they found that the population in-migration was exceeding out-migration, so they set out to find the reasons. Questionnaires were given to those who moved in and sent to those who moved out. They asked sex, marital status, age group, occupation, income level, and where moved to or from. One- to three-sentence answers were solicited for the following questions: (1) Why did you choose the area you have moved to? (b) Why did you choose to leave the area that you moved from? The answers were then grouped into general categories to see trends. *Do a similar study for your area.* (Note: age and income levels should be in broad ranges—some people do not like giving out their exact age or income.)

To take the study one step further, ask the new residents to list the things that they like best about the region and ask the long time residents what they feel the area needs. Often there is a strong contrast between these two lists. People who live in an area sometimes lose sight of their own community's values. Compare these two lists. Can all of the things on both lists be accomplished in this region? How would it change the general personality of the region?

COMMUNITY HEALTH

A community is a living entity and human beings are one of the components of the living mass. Like all organisms, disease, decay, and death are possible. Thousands of ghost towns and historic sites dot United States maps and indicate where people have lived in what they thought were permanent settlements.

These communities were often economic entities only and the reduction or elimination of their resource base destroyed the health of the whole. Sometimes the communities were artificial creations of government to hold ethnic populations during times of war or unusual stress situations like the Dust Bowl era. These temporary cities

There are many parallels between the natural and human communities.

often fail because they lack a history and do not reflect group beliefs or cultural uniqueness. They are too sterile.

Colin Turnbull, an anthropologist, gives us a glimpse of an extreme in community destruction in his book *The Mountain People,* which chronicles the life of the Ik, a people of Uganda. They were a hunter-gatherer society whose beliefs included an ethic that did not allow warfare or over-hunting. They lived in small bands spread over a large, fertile domain, and their only interactions were occasional group hunts.

They believed that they were at one with Mount Morungole and neither they nor their mountain could exist without the other. They developed ritual, tradition, belief, and values, which held the people together.

57

Under government order the bands were pushed together into a density, intimacy, and frequency of contact that exceeded anything that they had ever experienced, and they were required to become farmers rather than hunters.

The population changed from group living to individual survival, because the group was too large to be cohesive. Humanity reversed itself. Instead of open courtyards around each group of huts within the large compound, there was a maze of walls and tunnels, booby-trapped with spears. Homemaking deteriorated, feces littered doorsteps, adultery and incest taboos were broken, and marriage had no value.

A twelve year old retarded girl believed that food was for sharing and savoring, and her playmates beat her. She believed that parents were for loving and to be loved by, and to cure her madness she was locked in her hut until she died and decayed.

Laughter, that unique quality that belongs only to human be-

History need not be a mere process in memorization; it can be a participation subject as well.
COURTESY CRAIG R. BORCK.

ings, became the outstanding trait of the Ik village. An entire village would rush to the edge of a low cliff and join in a communal laugh as a blind old lady lay thrashing on her back, near death. A child crawled close to a fire, got burned, and set the whole group to laughter. Laughter was even shared as boys and girls gathered around an old man, too weak to walk, and pelted him with stones and sticks until he cried.

Turnbull concludes: *No human Nature?*

> The Ik teach us that our vaunted human values are not inherent in humanity at all, but are associated only with a particular form of survival called society, and that all, even society itself, are luxuries that can be dispensed with. That does not make them any the less so wonderful or desirable, and if man has any greatness, it is surely in his ability to maintain these values, clinging to them to an often very bitter end, even shortening an already pitifully short life rather than sacrifice his humanity. But that too involves choice, and the Ik teach us that man can lose the will to make it.

Activity

1.   Large cities often divided into ethnic blocks because immigrants found security in living with people of a similar background and language. Once begun it is difficult to break up ethnic areas because a sub-culture exists that makes new residents into outsiders or even invaders. Map the communities within your community. What are the qualities that make the neighborhoods unique? It is not racism to acknowledge the fact that races exist and have established some unique ethnocentricities.

2.   We often refer to cities by a unique quality or characteristic that they possess. How would you describe the towns in your county or state? Look for their uniqueness.

MAPPING COMPONENTS OF OUR COMMUNITY

Mapping is an important tool for analysis of a community. Maps are available from the county assessor's office, newspapers, U.S. Geological Survey (USGS), state highway departments, and the Soil Conservation Service. You are another source. A compass for direction, your pace for measuring distances, and some graph paper can provide the means for accurately recording information.

1.   Using available soil and topographic and community maps, make a large scale map of your community. Show buildings, green

areas, roads, railroads, and other surface details. Use sheets of clear plastic to make overlays showing slopes and soils.

2. Map underground things, including underground sewers and telephone and electrical lines, using surface clues. Contact the appropriate agencies to compare your map with theirs. Make an overlay of plastic for the underground information.

3. Map things you cannot see. For example: which way does the wind blow? Where does bad weather usually come from?

4. Map traffic flows. From sample counts determine the amount and direction of travel on streets and highways in your community. Do the same thing with foot traffic in the community and in the school building. Are there peak times of traffic during the day?

5. Map the businesses and residences. Show by color code where you buy goods, services, and entertainment, which are public buildings, which represent industry, and which represent cultural or spiritual services. Is there any pattern for the distribution of these components in the community? Can you determine a possible order for these buildings that would be more logical if you could start over?

One of the most visual and exciting projects is a scale model relief map. The map represents an exaggerated contour model of the area and can show plants, buildings, and any details your class wants. You must have two scales: the horizontal scale determines the area you want to cover, and can be defined according to your study; and the vertical scale relates to buildings, trees and elevation changes in the landscape. Since horizontal distances are much greater than vertical height variation, you want the vertical exaggerated, so that it will show up. In addition, your buildings will have to be tall enough to look like buildings.

Begin by drawing a city map complete with all the details you want to include. Make it the same size the final relief map will be. Use a U.S. Geological Survey (USGS) topographic map for land contours and draw them on the city map. This is the blueprint for your model.

Use ¾ inch plywood as the base for your model. This will allow you to pick up the map and move it without damaging the model itself. There are two methods for building up the contours. One method is plywood cutouts. This method is easy to use, but hard to describe. It involves layering plywood on plywood to make the relief model.

1. Use the plywood base to represent the lowest elevation in the community.
2. Cut out the lowest elevation from your paper blueprint and cut out pieces of plywood to match the remaining sections of the map.

3. Glue these sections in their proper location on the base map. This will now represent all areas that are at least as tall as the contour interval on the USGS map.

4. On your blueprint map cut out the remaining lowest elevation and make plywood cutouts to correspond to the map that you have left.

5. Glue these on to the two tiers of plywood that you have already glued.

6. Repeat this procedure until you have eliminated all the contours one at a time.

7. Paint on railroad tracks, highways, streams and vegetation.

8. Glue on trees and building models.

Another method is to use chicken wire, a fence mesh available at hardware stores, to create the contours that you want. It can be bunched, rolled, shaped, and stapled to the board.

1. Cover the mesh with strips of paper maché or use strips of cast tape (pre-packaged tape that has plaster of paris imbedded into the gauze). Wet it and lay it across the chicken wire to give a solid base.

2. Spread liquid plaster of paris over the entire surface and allow it to dry completely. This will give a smooth working surface.

3. Paint on appropriate roads and vegetation. Add twig trees, model buildings, and other details. Be creative.

Five

Outdoor Activities

An infant who has just learned to hold his head up has a frank and forthright way of gazing about him in bewilderment. He hasn't the faintest clue where he is, and he aims to learn. In a couple of years, what he will have learned instead is how to fake it: he'll have the cocksure air of a squatter who has come to feel he owns the place. Some unwanted, taught pride diverts us from our original intent, which is to explore the neighborhood, view the landscape, to discover at least *where* it is we have been so startlingly set down, if we can't learn why.

ANNIE DILLARD

Be creative! Attempt to teach every fact in an imaginative and un-forgettable way. Never accept the commonplace. Open eyes, introduce the students' senses to exhilarating experiences. Try lots of approaches, blend your personality with your lessons, and stay excited.

Outdoor experiences are minimal in relation to a person's overall experiences. There are exceptions, but most people spend most of their lives in one building or another. Calculate the amount of time spent in home, school, stores, church and institutions, and how much time is spent outside. Take the "outside" time and figure what part of it is spent in a vehicle. To complete the picture, figure out what activities are used for recreation. How many of them are done inside? The outdoor setting is important to our rest, relaxation, and sanity.

To create a good outdoor experience for your students, do those things with which you are most comfortable. Be inspiring and sell yourself. If a group believes in you, they will believe what you say. If a group is inspired by you, they will be inspired by what you show. If students respect you, they will want to do those things which please you. Nature will inspire and motivate people, but for many, you are the first bridge towards care and understanding.

Leading a Hike.   There is a man in California who has chosen not to talk anymore. He communicates with his banjo, his drawings, and his ability to listen. That works for him, but it will not work for all of us.

Some people are comfortable with the walk-and-lecture approach to a hike. This is a passive form of study for the group and can only be done when the group has a high degree of interest and has a very interesting leader. It is important to be entertaining as well as informative in this situation.

Pace depends on you and the individual group. Sometimes you will want to use a brisk, long walk to wear off the boisterous quality of a group. Be careful that it does not wear you down instead. Keep people actively involved.

A New Yorker who visits many new areas has a special technique for leading hikes in places he is unfamiliar with. He has the group determine what each person's strengths are and assigns them to be experts in that particular field. Then they all lead the hike.

The artist Reinhold P. Markhausen likes to take people on "finding" hikes. He says that there is a difference between finding and searching. If you are finding things, there can be many interesting objectives for you to observe. If you are searching, those interesting objects are bypassed because you are rejecting them in pursuit of a searched for object.

Answering Questions.   Many groups like the "answer a question with a question" method. When a member of the group asks a question, a question is given back to them in reply, making them search out the answer for themselves. It sounds good in theory, but be careful, most of the time this method is used incorrectly.

This technique should not be used to cover up for a lack of knowledge. This is intimidating and poor teaching. A person can only answer a question on the basis of what is already known. If the answer to your reply question requires more knowledge than the questioner has, that student will be unable to answer it, no matter how long you wait.

Be honest and admit when you yourself do not know the answer, then observe enough details to allow you to look up the answer when you get to a reference. This teaches methodical observation, and helps both student and leader learn something new.

We expect students to accept information that we dispense

without proof of any kind. "Well, kids, there are deer in the woods." There are, but how do they know? To make a fact pertinent, let the students determine it. An assignment should be to go out and prove that there are deer in the woods. The students should be given a ruler, paper and pencil, plaster of paris for track casting, and a container for scats. Are there really deer there? What is their proof?

Give an answer, plus a little more, and make the questioner feel happy that the question was asked. Talk about the plant or animal before or after giving it a name, but avoid sounding like you are reading the text from a field guide. Share your group's interests. Tell about Indian lore, herbal properties, wild foods, and unusual habits, in addition to the name.

Naming jewelweed is not sufficient. Touch the ripened seed pods and watch the seeds catapult away. Crush a stem and feel the liquid that is used to counteract the sting of bees, poison ivy, and nettle. Look at the trumpet-shaped flower. Hold the leaf under water and see the gold and silver shine where air is trapped on the leafy hairs.

Identifying a chickadee nest is not half as much fun as telling how the little bird will hiss like a snake and then throw his body against the side of the nesting cavity, like an uncoiling reptile.

If you have limited knowledge about the outdoors and want to take a group out anyway, use the theme "Teach the Teacher." Use your senses to get as many feelings as you can. Draw pictures, make maps, and take notes to remember. Proceed as though you were visitors from another planet and want to glean all the information you can from this strange place called Earth. Plan your trip at the launching pad. What will you take along? What will you look for? How will you make your investigations? Then gather your data and analyze and research it back at home base.

Themes. Establish a theme for your outing, such as senses, discovery, birds, leaves, or animal homes. Lead a "birdless" bird hike and attempt to learn as much as you can about where the birds are and what they do. The main rule is that no one may look at a bird.

Find bird signs, such as the distinctive holes that most woodpeckers make. Look for specific nests and the tracks of shorebirds and crows. Find raptor pellets and whitewash. Listen to the songs and calls and watch for shadows as the birds fly overhead. Feathers, food, egg shells, and animals that may eat birds are further possibilities for observation.

Aesthetics. Observe and become involved with aesthetics. Freeman Tilden, the developer of the National Park System Interpretive Program (and author of *Interpreting Our Heritage*), felt that the finest use of the system might be in a walk with beauty in which the interpreter was a humble companion sharing the adventure.

Aesthetics involve contemplation and admiration. It is an awareness of the surroundings and the awesome complexity of the universe, combined with humility in the observer. Poetic and artistic designs in nature captivate a person, while physical activities, like climbing and canoeing, put people into contact with aesthetic qualities. We gain aesthetic appreciation by looking, sensing, becoming involved. You can provide people with an opportunity to experience aesthetics, but aesthetics cannot be taught: it happens.

Frank Lloyd Wright wrote, "Hunt for the gray-green lichen clinging almost unnoticed to the rock! If you want to know the law of life, study the seashell's countless variations on a single theme: survival in a world of ceaseless movement."

Sit on a rock and watch a rainbow arch over a field after a refreshing rain. Paddle silently into the sunset. Ski over glittering snow crystals in the light of a full moon. Walk through crisp autumn leaves. Make a silent experience part of an intensive learning session if your group is ready for it.

Announce a daily sunset program and sit on the beach to watch the sun put on a one-performer show that varies each evening. If you want to give it a standing ovation on extraordinary evenings, by all means do so.

One nature center tried a brief experiment to determine what was aesthetic. They gave people a camera and instructed them to take pictures of what they liked. The pictures were then developed and given back to the photographers after the center had recorded what had been photographed. The nature center's marsh was the most popular subject.

Outdoor studies can be included in a homework assignment. They can be ongoing observations of such things as spring phenology, the sequence of events that happen each season. Certain birds migrate in ahead of others, certain flowers open before others. By simple observations and dated records you will be able to compare these annual events. A retired University of Minnesota professor has a thirty-five-year record of phenological events.

Research. If you can participate in projects that are current research, it will give the students a sense of accomplishment and purpose. The Cornell University Bird Nest Observation Program and the annual National Audubon Society Christmas Bird Count are good activities. Check with local organizations and universities to see where you might be able to assist them with one of their projects.

Try to give students a tangible conclusion to an elaborate study. Most often we do things to learn for ourselves, but occasionally we can do something more, like influencing legislation, or developing a personal lifestyle.

You might consider creating a time capsule that represents your environment. It could be used at a ten-year class reunion or for other classes.

Role Playing. Use role playing to understand complexity in the natural world. The activity may be designed to compare different human values for a resource like the wolf, a forest, or a lake. It can also be used to try to understand those things that are almost beyond comprehension, like size and distance.

Role playing is a very real method for illustrating and understanding nature. Northwoods Audubon Center stresses personal contact with the natural world and attempts to add the important third dimension to environmental education that cannot come through lecture, picture, or book. In some areas it has been successful in adding a fourth dimension through creative drama.

Have you ever been a migrating bird, a continental glacier, an orbiting planet, or a monarch butterfly? Think of a child, or even an adult, wrestling with the concept of a glacier and glacial landforms, or the concept of the universe. Can you really conceive of a wall of ice and snow and assorted debris, ten thousand feet tall, or one astronomical unit of 93 million miles?

It is much easier to understand the things that we can relate to and through the use of involvement (acting) students may be able to grasp ideas that would otherwise be alien to them.

For a study on birds, discussion might start with migration; to illustrate the migration patterns, two areas should be designated as the North and the South Poles respectively. Students should be assigned roles as various animal species in specific locations. The class should then move through the seasons with each bird going to assigned wintering spots. The students will be able to see some classmates standing still the entire time (non-migrant species), some traveling north to south (longitudinal migration), and a few traveling from east to west (latitudinal migration).

There will be variations in the general movement: the Hermann gull may go north while the rest go south (reverse longitudinal), a quail in California may go up and down a rock or stump (altitudinal), and, after several repetitions, the snowy owl may make a movement (sporadic). The students will know their own species for sure and will probably have a better grasp of the complexity of migration.

During this migration study you might also study caribou migrating across the tundra, salmon spawning up the coast and dying in the rivers, bats migrating to the south, and monarch butterflies going to Mexico. This will stress the fact that migration is more than just a bird phenomenon.

Role playing can be used in an astronomy lesson to experience the dimensions of our solar system. Use a 110 mm sun and assign planet names to individuals in the group. Then spread them out at distances proportional to the size of the planet they are holding. (A black dot or circle on a card can represent the size of the planet.) Place each planet in position and call out its name as you do so. Each intervening planet should also call out the last planet's name until the knowledge of that planet's placement reaches the Sun and its cohorts.

Once Pluto is positioned and announced, the leader returns to the Sun and neighboring nebula, inviting them to join an interplanetary flight to meet the solar system. Have each planet join the flight as you travel from planet to planet, moving from the Sun to Pluto. Use the following chart for your solar system model. If your group is large enough, you can also place the various moons in position as well. This activity can be done at night to add to the effect. Table 5.1 presents a scale model of planet dimensions.

Table 5.1. Solar System Model

Use a Sun with a diameter of 110 mm.		
Planets	Distance from Sun	Diameter
MERCURY	4 m	.3 mm
VENUS	7 m	.8 mm
EARTH	10 m	.8 mm
MARS	15 m	.4 mm
JUPITER	52 m	9.4 mm
SATURN	95 m	7.1 mm
URANUS	192 m	3.1 mm
NEPTUNE	301 m	3.0 mm
PLUTO	395 m	1.0 mm

Scale: 10 m = 93,000,000 miles, 1 m = 9,300,000 miles, 1 mm = 9,300 miles.

This activity stresses an understanding of the difficult concept of *millions of miles,* provides involvement, and establishes a feeling for a passive observation of the constellations.

The rich lore that transmits the beliefs of our early ancestors is tied to the names and formations of constellations and can be used to further relate the stars to the students. For example, the Milky Way was a road for dead Viking heroes to travel to Valhalla. It was also the route of the Indian warriors who built many fires on the way to their hunting grounds. In India it is considered to be a snake.

Value Clarification. Value clarification is a process of presenting the variables for a decision that allows the student to evaluate the options, make a decision, and determine action. Encourage your group to interact about good and bad. Let them make some judgments. The clarification of established values is your most important goal because it is values that will make that person want to preserve the things you are identifying and working with.

There is also a time to verbalize your own values. Do not be afraid to be assertive, occasionally your beliefs are important. Speak up when needed. You cannot make others share your feelings, but you can get them to think about your values and theirs.

Many educators frown on this process. They do not like to assert their leadership because they feel that it robs the students of a decision-making process, but in the naturalist field there is justification for this periodic dominance. The natural world does not have time to lose. There is not a day that goes by that some part of it is not being destroyed.

Valuing is a person decision-making process. Students must be given time to think about what they see.

Techniques for teaching vary with the individual. The rest of this chapter is devoted to ideas: things to do, and things to start you thinking. Share the ideas with others and add some of your own. This is just the beginning.

Sensory Experience.   Not all work in nature needs to focus on the proper name and identification of the object. Sometimes we must concern ourselves with feelings. One person may stand over a clump of lichens and be as excited as can be, while the next person may find the entire setting beautiful and the lichens themselves not so interesting. Therefore, we should not concentrate on telling people what is pleasant, beautiful, or exciting, but instead give that person the opportunity to discover these things alone.

Questions for Discussion

1.   How do we perceive the world?
2.   How is my world different from yours?
3.   What are the different ways which we communicate?
4.   Do other animals perceive the world differently than we do?
5.   Is 24 hours the ideal time sequence for all people?

Activities

1.   Discover a cubic foot. How many things can exist in this space?
2.   Look at an area blindfolded. Paint a picture of what you "saw" with your blindfold on. (This activity works well if the students can be taken to an area blindfolded, are given time to explore the area, and then are returned to a classroom (or outside area) to paint the picture, keeping their blindfolds on until they are away from their explored area. Then return them to their area to see what it really looks like.) Try drawing a picture of your area while you are still blindfolded.
3.   Record all sense experiences received in a ten minute period.
4.   Test your sense of smell. Use small containers, painted black so that you cannot see what is inside of each one.
5.   Taste wild edibles.
6.   Make a nature mobile.
7.   Be an animal and try to discover its world.
8.   Eliminate the use of one sense for a period of time. Try it with each of the senses.
9.   Pick something with texture and then concentrate on one square inch of it. Enlarge that one inch into one square foot by drawing a picture of what you see.
10.   Look at a tree blindfolded and then try to find it again without the blindfold on.

11. Map the mini-climates of an area using your senses instead of weather instruments.

12. Lie down on the ground and observe the world from that level. How do things appear? Take a photograph or draw a picture from that level.

Night Study.   Our view of night is tempered by the limitations of our senses and our imagination. Sight, in particular, is altered by the limited light; we have relied on our eyes to such an extent that we fear the loss of them and distrust situations that limit their use. The biggest problem of a night study, therefore, is overcoming that fear.

Questions for Study and Discussion

1.   What are the real dangers of night in the woods?

2.   What sounds do you expect to hear in the night?

3.   Is man nocturnal or diurnal? Why?

4.   What is the benefit of being nocturnal?

5.   What do plants do at night?

Projects

1.   Observe bats hunting insects.

2.   Take a silent group night hike. Use a rope with knots at ten foot intervals to maintain both distance and reassurance.

3.   Set up feeding stations with lights.

4.   Test night blindness. Place white poles at ten foot intervals and, from a designated spot, see how many can be observed. Repeat the test after being outside in the dark for an hour. Is there a difference? Why?

5.   Collect insects at night.

6.   Set up a light near a pond and see what amphibians are attracted to it.

7.   Assign students to be tape recorders. Have them sit out in the dark for a half-hour "recording" night sounds. Get the group together and "play back" all of the recorders.

8.   Paint night pictures using water colors and sketch pads. Paint in the dark, using no artificial lights.

9.   Sleep out under the stars.

10.   Take time exposure photographs.

11.   Listen to city sounds and identify them (try to discern cars from trucks) and prepare for a woodland experience.

12.   Use braille compasses for night orienteering. (Available from Silva Company, Highway 39 North, LaPorte, Indiana 46350.)

13. Do a 24-hour study. Every four hours have students check a variety of locations and record different data. This could include a plankton tow, a mammal live trap line, sound recordings, the attraction of insects with lights reflected on white sheets and light boxes, the sampling of insects with sweep nets and beat nets. Note temperature changes.
14. Fish for crappies in day time and night time. Why is there a difference?
15. Find spawning streams and observe night movements of fish.

ASTRONOMY

Astronomy is the oldest science in which man has delved and it is one which still leaves much to the imagination. Unlike many sciences, this area of natural history cannot be controlled or brought into the lab. This means that each person can enjoy the opportunity to look and wonder with the best.

Questions for Study and Discussion

1. What is the history of astronomy?
2. What is the difference between a planet and a star?
3. What is the sun?
4. How can we prove that the Earth is not the center of the universe?
5. What is the Zodiac?
6. How are distances measured to the stars?
7. Is there any other life in space? Does it matter?
8. What stories and legends are associated with the various stars and constellations?

Projects

1. Make up individual star charts. Lie on your back on the ground and draw what you see in the sky. Make up your own constellations and a story to go with them.
2. Make constellation cans by punching holes in the end of cans with different sized nails to represent the arrangement of the stars. Use the beam of a flashlight to project the constellations on a wall or piece of dark material.
3. Make a sundial and a shadow board. A shadow board is used to mark shadow length at the same time each day, thereby seeing the angle of the Sun change.

4. Make a simple sextant, the instrument used by sailors to determine latitude, using a straw, protractor, string, and fish weights. Attach the straw to the protractor base and a weight to the middle point with a string. View the North Star through the straw and determine latitude by the point where the string crosses the degree markings on the protractor.

Beginners should start on cloudless nights when the moon is between the crescent and first quarter. The moonlight during this period blots out thousands of confusing stars of the fifth magnitude and constellations show up more clearly.

A good way to observe the sky is to lie down in a canoe, watch the sun set, and the sky light up over the lake. The moon will be the first night sight if it is rising early, followed first by the planets which may be visible, then followed by the first magnitude stars, second, third, and on to the fifth magnitude. The night sky begins simply and gains complexity as time passes.

Binocular Sights in the Night Sky

1. The Beehive: a cluster in the midst of Cancer.
2. Cancer double and triple stars.
3. The Pleiades Star Cluster has only six stars visible to the naked eye, but the sky will light up with binoculars.
4. Andromeda Galaxy is the farthest point visible to the naked eye. Its galaxy shape becomes apparent in binoculars.
5. Hyades is a v-shaped cluster in Taurus. Many double stars are visible in binoculars, as well as the v-shape.
6. View the moon with binoculars and you will see craters and seas.
7. Jupiter is the best planet to observe with binoculars because it is possible to see its moons as well.
8. Saturn's rings may show up in high powered binoculars.

Sights Without Binoculars

1. Northern Lights: static electricity as photons from solar storms follow the paths of our magnetic field and ignite at the poles.
2. Winter Triangle: three bright first magnitude stars, Procyon (Canis Minor), Sirius (Canis Major) and Betelgeuse (Orion).

3. Three stars in a row in the winter sky: Orion's belt.
4. Spring in the western sky: the backward question mark in Leo.
5. Summer Triangle of first magnitude stars: Deneb (Cygnus), Vega (Lyra), and Altair (Aquila).
6. The "W" of Cassiopeia.
7. Square of Pegasus.
8. Big Dipper and the North Star.
9. Satellites moving quickly across the sky.
10. Moon dogs: a rainbow formed by the moon's reflected light in high altitude, cirrus clouds.
11. The Northern Cross (Cygnus).
12. The reflection of the sky on a clear lake.
13. Solar eclipse.

Table 5.2 lists the names of meteor showers along with other related information.

Table 5.2. Meteor Showers

Name	Radiant Constellation	Dates	Type of trail
Quadrantids	NE Bootes	Jan. 1–6	slow, long
Lyrids	Lyra, Hercules border	April 18–25	very bright, swift
Eta Aquarids (Best in south)	Aquarius	April 21–May 12	swift streaks
Delta Aquarids	Aquarius	July 27–Aug. 12	swift streaks, yellow
Capricornids	Capricorn	July 18–Aug. 25	bright fireballs
Perseids	Perseus-Cassiopeia	July 25–Aug. 20	swift streaks, fireballs, faint white-yellow bright green-orange
Draconids	Draco	Oct. 7–10	swift streaks
Orionids	Orion's Club	Oct. 19	swift streaks, most faint
Taurids	Taurus	Sept. 15–Oct. 15	slow, bright fireballs, two to fifteen per hour
Andromedids	Andromeda	Aug. 31–Nov. 29	bright, often red, trains of orange sparks
Leonids	Leo	Nov. 14–20	fastest streaks, some fireballs
Geminids	Gemini	Dec. 12	short paths, medium speed
Ursids (Best in north)	Ursa Minor	Dec. 17–24	medium speed, fairly bright

METEOROLOGY

What aspect of nature affects man more than the weather? Too much rain or too little, too much heat, too cold, too windy, or almost any "too" that you care to list regarding weather conditions can cause discomfort or destruction. The study of weather is an area in which everyone can gain some working knowledge with little trouble.

Questions for Study and Discussion

1. What creates winds?
2. How does weather influence the plant and animal worlds?
3. What is a warm front? What is a cold front?
4. What is air pollution?
5. How does weather shape the earth?

Projects

1. Make a weather station, including a rain gauge, wind vane, barometer, hygrometer, and thermometer.
2. Study winds in your area using helium balloons. Include post cards to be returned to you.
3. Check the dew point.
4. Check building smokestack emissions by using a Ringleman Chart.
5. Coat a jar with Vaseline and place it outside to catch particulate matter from the air.
6. Maintain records of weather and individual moods.
7. Use your senses to record hot, cold, muggy, windy, and dry. Compare with instrumental readings.
8. See the section on bad weather in Chapter 6.

Table 5.3 gives information about wind in its various degrees of intensity.

Weather Signs

When ye see a cloud rise out of the west, straightway cometh the rain; and so it is. (Luke 12:54)

It can be interesting to make your own weather predictions. Here are some hints to help you. Weather will generally remain fair when

Table 5.3. Beaufort Wind Scale

MPH	Description	Observation
0–1	calm	smoke rises vertically
1–3	light air	smoke drifts slowly
4–7	slight breeze	leaves rustle
8–12	gentle breeze	leaves and twigs in motion
13–18	moderate breeze	small branches move
19–24	fresh breeze	small trees sway
25–31	strong breeze	larges branches sway
32–38	moderate gale	whole trees in motion
39–46	fresh gale	twigs break off trees
47–54	strong gale	branches break
55–63	whole gale	trees snap and are blown down
64–72	storm	widespread damage
73–82	hurricane	extreme damage

1. the wind blows gently from west or northwest.
2. the barometer remains steady or rises.
3. cumulus clouds dot the summer sky in the afternoon.
4. morning fog breaks or "burns off" by noon.
5. there is dew on the ground.
6. mares tails are sparse and scattered.
7. clouds stay high and flow with prevailing winds.
8. smoke rises and disappears.
9. cloud base has hard, downward protuberances.

Rainy weather or snow may come when

1. cirrus clouds thicken and are followed by lower clouds with leaden bellies, particularly if barometer is dropping.
2. there is a ring around the moon, particularly if barometer is dropping.
3. puffy cumulus clouds begin to develop vertically.
4. sky is dark and threatening to the west.
5. southerly wind increases in speed with clouds moving from west.
6. the wind, particularly a north wind, shifts in a counter-clockwise direction, that is, from north to west to south.
7. the barometer falls steadily.
8. the birds are not flying as much as usual.

9. the birds congregate and gorge themselves at feeders and then disappear.
10. smoke curls downward.
11. cumulus clouds become tufted and lumped together.
12. there is a mackerel sky and cirrocumulus clouds.
13. needles of a pine tree turn west (folklore).
14. birds ruffle their feathers and huddle together.
15. swallows stay in their nest boxes.
16. cattle and horses stay in close groups.
17. ants carry their eggs deeper into the mound.
18. a bird's flight is low.
19. fish start biting with a sudden barometric change.
20. insects are more bothersome than usual.
21. human hair gets limp.

ROCKS AND MINERALS

A geologist can travel throughout the states looking at exposed bedrock formations, collecting and studying minerals. Most of your activities will necessarily be limited to a place nearby. In the northern areas this will be a glacial till and rock picking will be best at an exposed gravel pit.

Look at the rocks at the gravel pit with interest in color and shape, but do not think that you are going to be able to recognize all the rocks and minerals there. They do not look the same as polished specimens.

Questions for Study and Discussion

1. What is the difference between a rock and a mineral?
2. Where do rocks come from?
3. What effect do rocks have on life forms?
4. Why should rocks be split open for identification?
5. Are there rocks being formed today?

Projects

1. Make a collection of rocks found in your area and display them.
2. Make a chart of human mineral needs and display rocks that provide those minerals.

3.   Polish rocks.

4.   Make arrowheads and tools from rocks. Which rocks work best?

Hint.   Persistent rust stains can be removed by soaking rock in an oxalic acid solution (three ounces to one quart of water). Also, a sandbag makes a good support when chiseling a fossil from a rock. It holds the piece, yet gives enough to prevent cracks, and protects your work area's surface.

SOILS

Soils are the link between the living and the non-living. Soils are mixtures of inorganic and organic materials. They consist of weathered mineral matter, water, air, decaying organic matter (humus), roots, bacteria, fungi, and numerous invertebrate animals. Soils result from the combined effects of climate (water and air), geology (parent material), topography (erosion, etc.) and time.

Questions for Study and Discussion

1.   Discuss how climate, geology, topography, time, and plants affect soil and soil formation.

2.   What organisms might be found in the soil?

3.   What effect will heavily trampled areas have on the ability of soil to absorb water?

4.   Discuss the water-holding capabilities of different soils and their importance to plants.

5.   Discuss the value of plant cover for preventing erosion.

Projects

1.   Make a soil profile. Dig down to expose layers. Examine the soil's color, structure, and texture.

2.   Compare soils of different plant communities. How do they differ?

3.   Demonstrate the value of plant cover in preventing erosion. Expose an area of a slope and pour water down the hillside. Catch the runoff in a jar. Do the same with a grassy area. Compare jars.

4.   Separate soil organisms from the soil. Use a Berlese funnel or shake the soil through screen mesh.

5.   Use a gardener's soil test kit and sample different areas. See if you can find different plants that correlate with soil conditions.

6. Make soil pictures, like the Southwestern Indian sand pictures.
7. Collect natural clay to make pottery.

The color of soil often indicates the extent of humus. Hence, soils very low in organic matter are usually light colored. The structure of the soil refers to the arrangement of the soil particles. Soil structure may be classified as:

1. Granular (particles flocculated)
2. Blocky
3. Prismatic
4. Platz (particles sticking together in a horizontal plate)
5. Single grained (sands)
6. No structure (tightly packed clays)

A soil profile is a vertical cross section of a body of soil extending from the surface into the parent material underneath. Soil texture refers to the size of the soil particles and to the relative proportions of sand, silt, and clay in the soil. The sizes of the soil particles used in reference to soil texture are:

sand: 2.00—0.05 mm
silt: 0.05—0.002 mm
clay: less than 0.002 mm

The fertility, erosion, aeration, water intake, water supply, and power of soil is largely determined by the soil texture. Use the form on the opposite page to do a soil profile for your area; then make a sketch of it.

WATER

Water in its various forms and purities is familiar to all of us. Whether it be water of a lake, pond, swamp, river, or ocean, water is very much a part of our natural surroundings and is a medium to which we can easily relate.

Many of us are probably most familiar with the recreational values of water. We may swim, boat, canoe, or just enjoy the aesthetic values of a body of water. However, water is more than just a substance to enjoy. It is a medium on which all life depends. No plant or animal can exist without it.

Examine a few of the physical properties of water and find ways in which one body of water might differ from another.

```
SOIL PROFILE

Site Location:
Predominant Vegetation Types:
Soil Horizons:
    Organic Layers: thickness of organic material_____
                    color_____
                    smell_____
                    animals found_____

    "A" Horizon: top soil, usually dark color
                    thickness_____
                    color_____
                    smell_____
                    animals_____
                    other_____

    "B" Horizon: subsoil, zone of accumulation
                    thickness_____
                    color_____
                    smell_____
                    animals_____
                    other_____

    "C" Horizon: parent material
                    thickness_____
                    color_____
                    smell_____
                    animals_____
                    other_____
```

Questions for Study and Discussion

1. Why does ice float?
2. What is temperature layering in water? How does it affect the flora and fauna?
3. What is turbidity? How might it affect water quality?
4. How might the land bordering an aquatic area affect water quality?
5. Why do some lakes support more extensive fauna populations than others?
6. Why are some lakes weedier than others?
7. How do some animals survive without taking a drink?

1. Make and use a secchi disk (a device which is lowered into the water to determine sunlight penetration).
2. Measure the turbidity and color of various aquatic environments.
3. Make a water sampler and sample lakes at various depths. Compare water samples from different lakes. Compare water samples from the same lake at different times of the year.
4. Record the temperature of various depths within a pond or lake.
5. Measure the water's pH.
6. Test the amount of CO_2 in the water.
7. Make a bottom dredge and take bottom samples.
8. Determine the rate of flow in a stream.
9. Map a lake basin or watershed.
10. Measure the volume of water coming into and leaving a lake. Is there a difference? Where does it go?
11. Make a benthos sampler. Put it out for a week or longer to let organisms colonize it. Bring it in and see what is living on it. A benthos sampler is any platform which can be placed on the bottom of a lake for colonization and can be retrieved for examination. Remember to put a float or buoy to mark the location and facilitate retrieval.
12. Take plankton samples in the weeds, in the open water, and at various depths. Try to see dispersion.
13. Make a plant aquarium.
14. Make an aquatic insect aquarium. Whirligigs and water striders are active surface insects that can be fed flies.
15. Look for exoskeletons from emerged insects.
16. Seine a pond for insects.
17. Observe dragonflies. Why are they called "mosquito hawks"?

Determining the Volume of Water Flow in a Stream

Select a section of the stream about ten feet long with rather uniform depth and width. Use the following formula to determine the rate of flow in cubic feet per second.

$$r = \frac{wdal}{t}$$

r = the rate of flow in cubic feet per second
w = average width of the channel in feet
d = the average depth in feet

a = a value of 0.8 if the stream bottom consists of loose rocks and coarse gravel or a value of 0.9 if the stream bottom is smooth (mud, sand, hardpan, or bedrock)

l = the length in feet of the channel section

t = the average time (make three tests) for a float to travel down the channel section.

If the stream flow is less than one cubic foot per second, convert to gallons per minute: 1 cubic ft/second = 450 gallons/minute.

Plant Zones of a Pond

1. An *emergent* plant zone is located closest to the store. It is dominated by plants that are rooted to the bottom and have stems and leaves above the surface. Grasses, sedges, and rushes are plants typical of the emergent zone in ponds and lakes. Many kinds of frogs, birds, and mammals find food and shelter in this zone. A variety of algae, protozoans, worms, insects, snails, and small fishes live among underwater plant stems.

2. A *floating leaf* plant zone: broad, flat-leafed water lilies and such floating plants as water ferns and duckweeds.

FISH

When we study aquatic environments and their indigenous populations, most people automatically think of fish. This correlation is largely a result of the popularity of sport fishing. Many of us have sat patiently for hours by a stream or lake trying to outwit those critters that swim beneath. Some have more success than others, but to all who have shared in such an experience, most recall a very memorable outing.

Fish make up the largest group of vertebrates. About 3,300 species are found in North American fresh and salt waters.

Questions for Study and Discussion

1. How do fish swim?
2. How do fish breathe?
3. What do fish eat? How do they detect their food?
4. Where are the most fish found within a lake or a river?

81

Projects

1. Seine an area and examine the species found.
2. Make a minnow trap.
3. Put out minnow traps and examine the catch.
4. Produce an ink and cloth print by wiping the oil off the fish, coating it with black ink, and covering it with a soft cloth to absorb the print.
5. Determine the age of fish by examining the scales.
6. Construct an aquarium.
7. Dive and observe fish in their natural habitat.

Method for Aging Fish: Scale Method

1. With a knife, scrape away about a dozen scales from the region behind the gill cover and above the pectoral fin.
2. Measure the length of the fish from tip of snout to end of tail and record. Fish may be returned *Live* to water.
3. Record other data, such as, location of catch, time of catch, date, weight of fish, sex of fish, and habitat.
4. Soak scales in clean water for about an hour. Scrub with an old toothbrush or scrape the surface with a toothpick.
5. Scales may be mounted permanently on a glass microscope slide. A mounting media may be obtained from biological supply houses. A temporary mount requires only a glass slide, drop of water, and a cover glass.
6. Examine under a microscope (low power, 40–50X) or magnifying glass.

Development of the scale. The focus is the first part of the scale to be developed. As the scale continues to grow, ridges surrounding the focus are laid down. These ridges are called circuli, and are rapidly laid down during the growing season (spring and summer), but development is slow in the fall and stops completely during the winter. When rapid growth starts in the spring, a rather discontinuous ridge becomes apparent. This is called the annulus or year mark and is the structure used in aging the fish.

BOTANY

Wildflower Study

Throughout the spring and summer each week brings new plants to flower and, eventually, to seed. The flowering plants are spermatophytes, or seed producers. Flowers can be annual, biennial, or perennial. They can also be herbaceous or woody plants.

82

The study of flowers should do more than just emphasize the name of the plant. Flowers should be studied as a part of the whole scheme of nature.

Questions for Study and Discussion

1. What eats flower seeds?
2. How do flowers reproduce?
3. How do flower seeds travel?
4. Why don't all flowers grow in the same places?
5. Why do flowers come in different colors?
6. What is the purpose of the flower's color?

Projects

1. Draw pictures of flowers that are common in your area. Make your own field guide.
2. Count the seeds of some plants and discuss what would happen if all of the seeds grew to be flowers.
3. Experiment with seedlings and see if they will grow in the shade. What does the plant do when you turn the pot?
4. Try growing the same type of seeds in different soils and keep a record of the growth.
5. Compare annual, perennial, and biennial plants.
6. Make a bulletin board of flowers in your area using drawings. Mark their blooming dates.
7. Watch flowers being pollinated, particularly milkweed plants.
8. Lick the dew from milkweed flowers: notice their sweetness. Use a pin to remove a pollen saddlebag from the flower.
9. Run through a field and see how many seeds you collect on your clothing.
10. Make twine out of wood nettle, sedge, or cordgrass, using Native American techniques.

Warning.   Some plants are protected by law and should be left alone. Never pick more flowers than you need for a specific study. A flower looks better growing than it does sitting in a glass on a table. If you have to pick flowers, leave the foliage if possible. Some plants take many years to go from seed to flower. In some orchids the time span is 20 years and in trillium it is six. Leave these plants in the wilds.

Hint.   Bolting and blooming in such biennials as mullein can be induced by placing the rosettes in temperatures just above freezing for one week.

WILD EDIBLES

A weed is just a plant whose virtues have not yet been discovered. For virtues we can list beauty, design, scent, and edibility. Wild edibles offer a chance to teach terminology and taxonomy. For a limited area and large groups, foraging must be limited to sampling and not overuse.

The emphasis must be on knowing the plants and not tasting unidentified plants. The following terms must be learned for an understanding in edible plants.

1. leaf
2. flower
3. seed
4. root
5. bud
6. shoot
7. tuber
8. stalk
9. bulb
10. fruit

Questions for Study and Discussion

1. What plants grow in your area?
2. How do the different habitats affect the plant variations?
3. What effect would sprays have on the edibility of wild plants?
4. How do the plants reproduce?
5. What animals eat plants?
6. How do plants fit into the food chain in nature?
7. What benefits, besides food, are derived from plants?
8. What did the American Indian eat in this area?

Projects

1. Make a bulletin board of pressed edibles.
2. Have a "taste of the week" with a bite of one different edible each week. Discuss other uses of the same plant.
3. Make a list of plants in one area: plants that we can eat; plants that birds eat; plants that other mammals eat; and other values of the plants.
4. Plant the seeds of some wild edibles in pots and grow where they can be observed.

Wild foods are more than a taste treat—they are a history of humanity and our relation to the wilds.

5. Discuss common vegetables and show what part of each is eaten (roots, bulb, leaves, seeds).

6. Study the origin of common vegetables.

7. Study the non-edible plants so that you will be able to know the differences.

8. Find out which garden plants are poisonous and which are edible.

Hint. Never compare a wild food with a garden vegetable. If you say a plant "tastes like . . .", people will be more intent on making the comparison than learning the new taste.

The following rules for foraging for wild foods are from *Grazing*, by Mike Link, published by Voyageur Press.

1. Know your plant and how to prepare it. Some are edible only if prepared in a certain way.

2. Know how abundant your plant is and take only one out of ten.

3. For every edible plant you learn, learn one poisonous or noxious plant.

4. Learn and try one plant at a time before experimenting.

5. Eat a little at a time. Each person reacts differently to foods and some plants may be perfectly edible, yet may cause a reaction for you.

6. Know what part of your plant is edible. The petiole on the rhubarb is edible, but the leaf is poisonous.

7. Start with the most common—dandelion, cattail, burdock, nettle—and see what you can do with them.

8. Observe nature as you are gathering. You might find out some very interesting things.

9. Do not gather along roadsides where herbicides may have been sprayed. Beware of pesticide spraying too.

10. Select the healthiest looking specimens. Avoid those which show discoloration or obvious insect infestation.

11. Do not expect your wild plant to taste like another food. There may be flavor similarities, but all foods taste like themselves. If you want something that tastes like tomatoes and peanut butter, then eat tomatoes and peanut butter, but don't eat wild foods looking for that flavor.

Herbs

The term "herb" as used here means plants with medicinal, magical, or utility value, rather than non-woody plants. The cuttings and seeds of the herbs were carried from east to west by our ancestors in their wanderings and with the plants came the myths and legends about them.

When we read about how herbs have been used from the earliest times until now, we learn about people's diets, their illnesses and their cures, their wounds and infections, their fears and superstitions. It is a way to study the intimate and personal side of history.

The science of chemurgy (investigation of uncultivated plants) is still in its infancy. The vegetable kingdom remains virtually unexplored and holds promise for new researchers.

For centuries the Greek shepherds dressed infected wounds with molds that grew on their long beards, and this led to the discovery of penicillin. We still have more to learn.

The ancient herbalist is the cultural ancestor of today's pharmacy.
COURTESY DAVID J. EAGAN.

Your study of herbs can be fun, but do not experiment with herbals. Do not remove all of your plants from the woods, for they look much better alive. In addition, some herbs are deadly poisons and the wrong use can be dangerous. Many of the things we find in ancient herbals have since been proven erroneous.

Questions for Study and Discussion

1. What is the "doctrine of signature"? Was it valid?
2. What parts of herbs are used for medicines?
3. What are other uses for plants?
4. Why were many herbalists considered to be witches?
5. What did your local Indian tribes use for medicine?
6. Do the plants have medicinal properties for the wild animals?

Projects

1. Make dyes from plants. Dye yarn, and weave, knit or crochet.
2. Make a bulletin board display of herbs and their uses.
3. Make a love potion. Old herbals are on the market and contain many ideas.
4. Make a local herbal with home remedies from your community. *Do not prescribe from it.*

Trees

Trees are the most advanced form of plant evolution. They are flowering plants that produce woody tissue and continue to grow year after year. Trees provide us with commercial products, as well as aesthetic, pleasure; trees also provide homes, food, shelter, shade, nutrients, and beauty for other life forms.

Activities, like *Adopt-a-Tree,* are processes of interaction between people and their environment.
COURTESY DAVID J. EAGAN.

Trees can be divided into two groups: trees and shrubs. Shrubs usually do not attain heights greater than fifteen feet, while some taller trees will reach into the sky for more than 300 feet.

Because of their many properties and many uses, trees are an important factor in the lives of mammals, birds, insects, and some reptiles and amphibians.

Questions for Study and Discussion

1. Of what value is a tree? (commercially and aesthetically)
2. What other life forms use trees? In what ways?
3. How does human activity affect trees?
4. How do trees grow? What do they need for growth?
5. How do trees reproduce?
6. What would the Earth be like without any trees?

Projects

1. Make a twig collection.
2. Make leaf prints using stamp pads.
3. Adopt a tree.
4. Mount pressed leaves.
5. Make spatter paintings of leaves.
6. Make seed collections.
7. Make a mobile using parts of a particular tree (twig, leaf, seed).
8. Investigate a stump or rotting log for life. Pick only one log and put it back together when you have completed your study of it.
9. Make birch baskets or small scale canoes. (Go to a logging area for materials.)
10. Make twine from elm or basswood inner bark.
11. Make baskets from oak or black ash wood.

Adopt a Tree. Assign students to pick a tree they like and to adopt it for a while. Ask them to make a booklet about their tree. Include a bark rubbing, using charcoal, pastels or crayon, a drawing of their tree, showing nests and other animal signs, a Haiku or poem about their tree, and leaf prints and seed prints. This can all be done on one sheet of paper that has been folded in half, putting the bark rubbing on the front for the cover.

Ferns

The study of ferns is really the study of leaves. Thoreau said that the reason ferns were made was to have perfect leaves.

Questions for Study and Discussion

1. How does a fern reproduce?
2. Where does the fern fit into the plant kingdom?
3. Is the stalk that you see above the ground really the stem of the fern?

Projects

1. Make one collection of leaves for the entire class.
2. Press the leaves.
3. Identify the fern and learn what type of leaf it is, pinnate or entire.
4. Collect one grouping of fiddleheads in early spring to observe them unfolding, and then place them back where you found them.
5. Make leaf prints using ink and paper.
6. Sow fern spores.

    a.   Sterilize small clay flowerpots in boiling water for twenty minutes.

    b.   Cool and fill with sphagnum moss, through which boiling water has been poured.

    c.   Invert in the bottom of a quart jar.

    d.   Sow spores on clay pot, and put a little bit of water in the bottom of the jar. Cover.

    e.   Set out of sun at room temperature.

    f.   In a few weeks you will see prothallium: the beginning fern form. If you maintain proper growing conditions a while longer, sporophyte will form. Pick off and plant in a woodland soil.

Warning: Be careful that you do not choose the activities that eliminate a species of fern from the woods. There will only be a limited amount of ferns, no matter how thick they look to you.

BIRD STUDY

Birds are in the class Aves and are differentiated from other animals by their feathers, flight, and incubation of eggs. They are fun to study because they are cheerful, colorful, and, most important, they are plentiful and easy to observe.

A bird study should emphasize how the birds fit into our total picture of nature. Relate birds to the different places in the food chain, and to the different habitat requirements. There are 1,780 species of birds in the world; 645 species, and 75 families in the United States.

Northwoods Audubon Center has accumulated data on the movement of evening grosbeaks in relation to weather systems.
COURTESY OF CRAIG R. BORCK.

Questions for Study and Discussion

1. What do birds eat? Why?
2. How do the shapes of birds' bills relate to their food?
3. Where are birds found?
4. What effects do humans have on the bird populations?

Projects

1. Set up a bird activity area. Make feeders, houses, and birdbaths. Clean regularly to prevent the transmission of disease.
2. Build a blind near a pond for observation.
3. Maintain a list of observations.
4. Collect wild seeds and seeds from the table (apple, grapefruit) and see which are eaten by the birds.
5. Make a bulletin board showing common birds and where they can be found.
6. Take a birdless bird hike. Find clues, such as nests, woodpecker holes, owl pellets, to show evidence of where birds have been without actually seeing the birds.
7. Use recordings to call in birds.
8. Make recordings of bird songs and calls.
9. Work with a bird bander.
10. Do a road side count of pheasants while on the school bus. Do it using sight and sound.

11. Make a census of ruffed grouse drumming in an area.

12. Observe woodpecker holes and look for tree species preferences.

13. Watch easily-observed birds for behavior differences as the weather changes.

14. Make a bird feeder census on the same days each year and compare.

15. Study a particular bird and make a nest out of the materials that would be used by that bird.

16. Study birds using the "Bird Study Sheet".

Red-Winged Blackbird Nesting Behavior Study

1. Observe a cattail marsh area and map the territories established by the birds. Red-wings will mark their territories by flying from plant to plant and singing their "con-quer-ree" song. The map should show positions of all other animals, as well as the red-wings.

2. What happens when territorial neighbors come in contact with

```
BIRD STUDY SHEET

Size:
    robin or smaller ____
    larger than a robin, but smaller than a crow ____
    crow size or larger ____

Where was it? _____

What was it doing? _____

Give it a descriptive name: _____

Prominent features: _____

Describe the bill: _____

Describe the feet: _____

Describe the song: _____

Observer: _____  Date: _____
```

each other? How do they avoid contact? Is there interaction between red-wings and other animals?

3. Observe an individual bird's reaction to a red-wing cardboard cutout placed on a stake within an identified territory. Play a tape recorder with a cassette of red-wing calls. Record observations. *Do not repeat this too often as it may upset the birds' breeding success.*

4. Return to the area with waders and locate the birds' nests. The adults will fly back and forth from the site when building the nest and when feeding the young. By observing this behavior, you can zero in on the nest location.

5. Do not destroy the nest or stay in the area for too long a time. Record height from ground, number of nests per territory and per square meter of territory, kind of vegetation, and height of vegetation on which the nest is found.

6. Place a camera on the nest and take a picture straight up. Use a grid overlay for the screen if slides are taken or for the snapshot. Count the number of grids covered with vegetation and calculate the percent of cover protecting the nest.

7. Check the nest on a weekly basis and keep a Cornell University Nest Record Card for each location. The Laboratory of Ornithology, Cornell University, Ithaca, New York, provides cards for recording nesting observations and maintains a computerized file of this information for researchers.

Nests and Eggs

Birds and mammals are thought to be direct descendants of the reptiles. Some scientists believe that the bird is a form of dinosaur. The Pteranadon is a flying lizard from which birds began to evolve. Like the lizard, the bird lays eggs and makes nests, although scientists suspect that during early evolution periods lizards dropped eggs as they flew over the land.

Questions for Study and Discussion

1. How do reptile and bird eggs compare?
2. What kind of care does a mother reptile give its young compared to the care given by a bird? Is there a reason for the difference in care?
3. Are there birds that do not care for their eggs?

Projects

1. Try using natural materials to construct a nest. Compare your results with an actual nest.

2. Use nest cards from Cornell Laboratory for observations. (see Red-Winged Blackbird number 7)

3. Make a nest observing pole with a two way makeup mirrror (one side magnifying) for best results.

4. Make an incubator and hatch chicken eggs.

5. Make a bulletin board showing birds, their nests, and their eggs.

Warning: Tampering with nests can chase off parents and leave a human scent for predators to follow. Be careful.

Bird Baths

1. Depth of water should be graduated from nothing at the edge of the pool or bath to not more than two and one-half inches at its deepest. Larger ground pools may be graduated up to twice the latter depth.

2. The bath must be swept or sponged out daily, or as often as it becomes defouled.

3. The inside of the bath should be rough. Coarse sand should be provided.

4. Bath should be emptied and allowed to sit dry in the sun for two days each week to kill bacteria.

5. If on or near the ground, no shrubbery or other possible concealment for cats should be within 25 feet of the bath. It is also a good idea to have some branchy tree within a few yards of the bath or pool so that the bathers, when alarmed, may easily reach a place of safety while their wet plumage dries. It can be a handicap in longer flights.

Table 5.4 gives specifications for building a bird house.

Table 5.4. Bird House Specifications

Species	Height Above Ground (feet)	Floor of Cavity (inches)	Depth of Cavity (inches)	Entrance Above Floor (inches)	Diameter of Entrance (inches)
Bluebird	5–10	5 × 5	10	8	1½
Chickadee	6–15	4 × 4	8–10	6–8	1⅛
Nuthatch	12–20	4 × 4	8–10	6–8	1¼
House Wren	6–10	4 × 4	6–8	1–6	1–1¼
Tree Swallow	10–15	5 × 5	6	1–6	1½
Purple Martin	15–20	6 × 6	6	1	2½
Crested Flycatcher	8–20	6 × 6	8–10	6–8	2
Flicker	6–20	7 × 7	16–18	14–16	2½
Downy Woodpecker	6–20	4 × 4	9–12	6–8	1¼
Hairy Woodpecker	6–20	6 × 6	12–15	9–12	1½
Kestrel	10–30	8 × 8	12–15	9–12	3
Wood Duck	10–20	10 × 18	10–24	12–16	4

MAMMALS

For some inexplicable reason, the word "animal" in common language is often restricted to the mammals. As a matter of fact, the bird, the fish, the insect, and the snake have just as much right to be called animals as has the chipmunk or the deer. A child should see how the fish differs from the bird and how the toad differs from the snake. Then it will be easy for them to grasp the fact that the mammals differ from all other animals. Children should also see how animals are alike. When they understand this, they will be able to comprehend how such diverse forms as the whale, cow, bat, and human are related.

Questions for Study and Discussion

1. What is a mammal?
2. How do mammals differ from one another?
3. What do mammals eat?
4. How do mammals protect themselves?
5. How do mammals spend the winter?
6. Can mammals fly? Can mammals swim under water?

Projects

1. Make a list of mammals in your state.
2. Make can live traps.
3. Establish a live trapline.
4. Make track castings (positive and negative).
5. Age a track: watch it on a daily basis and note changes.
6. Put track casts into a cloth bag and try to identify them by touch.
7. Observe mole tunnels in lawns.
8. Pretend to be a mammal other than human.
9. Record, describe, and sketch mammals.
10. Set up feeder areas: day and night.
11. Determine deer populations by pellet counts.

Tin Can Live Trap. To make a simple can live trap, fasten a piece of ¼ inch mesh hardware cloth to the rectangular bar on a mouse trap with a piece of wire. Then fasten the mouse trap to a #10 can with duct tape so that the mesh will cover the mouth of the opened end of the can when the trap is sprung.

Live Trapping Mammals: Important Rules

1. Inspect traps immediately in the morning and several times a day during hot and cold weather periods.
2. Keep traps out of direct sunlight whenever possible. This is especially important when metal traps are used.

3. Provide pieces of cotton or cloth inside the trap to be used as nest material in cold weather.

4. Use markers to show the location of your traps and make a map indicating the placement of all traps.

5. Number the traps to make sure they are all checked and collected after the study has been completed.

6. A permit is required to trap most of the larger mammals, but there are no restrictions on the smaller rodents. Check the rules for your state. Stress the fact that you are LIVE trapping and will be releasing the animals unharmed.

7. Look at the animal and release it ALIVE and in its own habitat. Do not handle the animals. Your scent might attract predators or warn prey and damage the animal's ability to survive.

8. Do not let students take the traps home. They are for study only. Animals have rights too.

Some Hints on Live Trapping

1. Study mammal signs (runways, droppings) in order to determine the best locations for setting traps.

2. Age new traps outside or bury them to remove fresh odors.

We are surrounded by common mammals that we recognize easily, but know very little about.
COURTESY CRAIG R. BORCK.

3. Small mammals may be placed in a quart jar for observing and identifying before releasing. Do not screw on a cap and cause suffocation of the animal.

4. Baits and Methods

    a. oppossum: dog food, fish, chicken entrails, table scraps

    b. mole: difficult to capture in live traps

    c. shrew: pitfall trap

    d. bat: mist net, removal from caves

    e. rabbit: apple, fresh vegetables

    f. muskrat: scented bait, fish, meat scraps, fresh vegetables

    g. porcupine: carrots, rutabagas

    h. mice, rats, etc.: small mammal mixture (see below)

    i. chipmunks, ground squirrels: small mammal mixture, sunflower seeds, peanuts

    j. tree squirrels: corn, nuts, sunflower seeds, small mammal mixture

    k. flying squirrels: small mammal mixture, apples, sunflower seeds

    l. woodchuck, marmot: stringbeans, corn, lettuce, apple, potato

    m. bear: dog food, meat scraps, fruits

    n. raccoon: dog food, meat scraps, fruit

    o. weasels, skunks: dog food, chicken bones and entrails, scraps

    p. fox, wolf, coyote: scented baits, dog food, meat scraps

    q. bobcat: catfood, dogfood, meat scraps, scented bait

    r. deer: salt block, scents, apples

    s. beaver: fresh aspen bark and leaves, scents

Small Mammal Mixture.

1 part melted suet (or use fat from cooking)
1 part peanut butter
1 part oatmeal
Mix well and store in a covered container in the refrigerator.

Deer Signs. The information gathered from the following questions and suggested actions will either prove or disprove that deer exist in the area surveyed:

If there are tracks in the area, sketch them.

Measure the track: What is the width? What is the length?

Measure the set of tracks: What is the width? What is the length?

List plants browsed on. How do you know it was deer browsing?

If there are pellets, sketch them. Indicate size of pellets.

What are some other signs?

Pellet Count to Determine White-Tailed Deer Populations

$$\text{Deer Per Square Mile} \times \frac{A\ (64{,}000)}{B\ (12.7)}$$

A   = average number of pellet groups per 11.8 foot radius plot

64,000 = number of plots that would fill one square mile

B   = number of days since leaves have come off trees

12.7   = number of pellet groups per day per deer

1. Set out on straight line bearings through study area.
2. Stop and count the number of pellet groups within a plot every 200 feet. Do not count any covered with leaves or outside of the circle.

The ecology of an area is the combination of its flora, fauna, weather, and geology, and how they interact.

3. Use a string 11.8 feet long to maintain a circle.

4. The more plots you have, the greater your accuracy.

Tracking Unit. Information gathered from the following questions and suggested actions will aid in determining what animals are in a particular area.

Draw pattern of the track observed.

How deep were the tracks? Are they fresh tracks or old tracks? How can you tell?

Measure width of one foot. What is the length?

Measure width of track from outside left foot to outside right foot.

Measure length of track, right front to right rear, and left front to left rear.

Describe the area where the track was seen.

Describe any variations in the pattern.

Draw any variations you may see.

Did you see any signs other than footprints?

What was the animal doing?

What animal was it?

Beaver Pond Study

1. Map the entire location.

2. Mark dam, lodge, scent mounds, cuttings, tracks, sightings, channels, secondary dams that slowed the water flow to allow the building of the main dam, and sink holes for escape. Lodge and dam construction should be studied. Make a very accurate map of the dam, noting each angle. Note the plants and animals that are around the pool. Do they differ from the rest of the area? Why?

3. Build a model of the flowage complex.

4. Look for evidence of what the area used to look like. Where was the main channel? Look for dead alders and willows in the pool, since they are usually stream shore plants. Note the dam's angles. A dam is usually pointed upstream at the main flow. The following diagram shows why. The flow in "A" keeps the dam closed; in "B" it will wash away. In "A" the flow forces the sides to push against each other.

5. Visit an abandoned dam site and try to predict what the area will be like in fifty years. Why would the beaver leave?

6. Look at stumps and identify the tree species that the animal has taken. Compare this with the dam and lodge materials and older

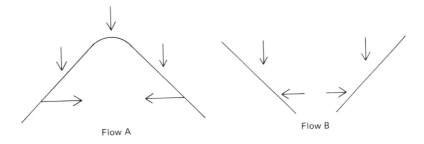

Flow A

Flow B

stumps. Has the beaver changed tree species? How much of the preferred tree species is left?

7. How old is the dam complex? Use an increment bore to drill the trees and count the rings to determine age. Age the trees along the edge of the dam. The growth will change where more sun is available. See drawing.

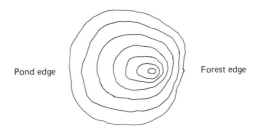

Pond edge

Forest edge

The tree cross section above is probably from a dam that is three or four years old, for that is when more sunlight was allowed to hit the tree and rings became larger on the side towards the pond. Do not do this in a major cutting area, since removal of trees later than the dam construction could also influence growth.

8. Take a boring on trees further inland to see how much the permanent water has influenced the border trees' growth.

9. Cut a tree that is standing dead in the pond and study its tree rings. How long did it live in water? Compare the ring size with living trees of the same species. Subtract the age of the pond from the living species to see how the rings compare. Was there a change in the last one to three rings of the dead tree?

10. Beavers have regular routines. At dust each evening they check their dams to see if repairs are needed, then they go after food. If you disrupt the dam just enough to necessitate minor repairs by the beaver, you can use a blind and a light with a red filter to observe their activity. The red light is not visible to them.

11. Note behavior patterns, such as the tail slap when they are startled. Make plaster casts of beaver tracks and note the sweet odor of the scent mounds.

12. Map signs of other animal species. How do they use the beaver area?

13. Sediment study: take soil profiles across the reservoir bottom. Muck should be thick towards the stream bed. Profile should show gravel in the old stream bed. See drawing.

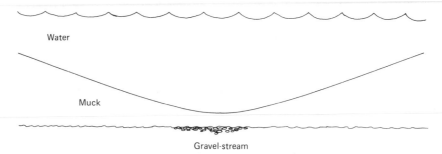

Gravel-stream

14. Calculate the beaver cuttings per week. Include tree species, tree thickness, and distance from water. Mark all the cuttings in the area and record and mark additional cuttings each week.

15. Establish a series of transect lines across an abandoned reservoir and map vegetation to determine succession patterns. Include both wood (species) and non-woody (type).

REPTILES AND AMPHIBIANS

Over the years people have generally tended to neglect the reptiles and amphibians. We know that people cannot get warts from handling toads and we realize that the stories about snakes with supernatural powers are not true. The stories or misconceptions that people have about reptiles and amphibians must be rectified before a successful study of them can be made. Once the fears are eliminated, an openminded study of this portion of the fauna can be made and their importance and role within the total ecosystem will be appreciated.

Questions for Study and Discussion

1. What is a reptile? What is an amphibian?

2. When, where, and how do we find them?

3. How do reptiles and amphibians protect themselves?

4. How do reptiles and amphibians spend their winter months?

5. What do they eat?

6. What is their role in the ecosystem?

7.   What "critters" are found in your area?

8.   Discuss fears and common superstitions associated with snakes and toads.

Projects

1.   Make a list of reptiles and amphibians in your area.

2.   Collect some frog or toad eggs and watch their development in an aquarium.

3.   Conduct a reptile and amphibian hunt. Study the live specimens and then release them back into their habitats.

4.   Discuss the proper care of reptiles and amphibians and demonstrate the building of enclosures for them.

5.   Set a gas lantern by the edge of a pond. What is attracted? Do frogs and toads come to feed?

6.   Listen to and make your own sound recordings of toads and frogs.

7.   Make clay models of reptiles and amphibians.

8.   Have frog jumping contests. (Read Mark Twain's short story, "The Notorious Jumping Frog of Calavers County.")

INSECT STUDY

For some reason people do not think of insects as animals, yet this group makes up ninety percent of all of the living creatures on earth. Perhaps this failure to identify them with the more familiar and higher forms of animals is because insects are strange and alien to our concept of the world. An insect in the adult stage is a small animal with six legs and three distinct body parts (head, thorax, abdomen). Nearly all insects have a pair of antennae and most have wings. Two pairs of wings are the rule, except for the Diptera (flies) which have only one pair.

Insects are the most numerous of all animals in both number of species and in total numbers. They are the most adaptive form of life in evolutionary history.

Questions for Study and Discussion

1.   What is an insect?

2.   Why isn't a spider an insect?

3.   How are crayfish related to insects?

4.   What is metamorphosis?

5.   How do insects affect plants?

6.   What kinds of homes do insects make?
7.   What are the good features about insects?
8.   Why do people in some countries eat insects?
9.   Why do we keep requiring stronger and stronger pesticides?

Projects

1.   Make one insect collection for the entire group representing the families found in your area.
2.   Make insect nets, insect cages, kill jars, and spreading boards.
3.   Make a formicarium to observe ant activities.
4.   Make a metamorphosis chart illustrating the changes that various insects go through.
5.   Make a bulletin board showing the various insect families.
6.   Observe ambush bugs and other insects in nature without disturbing them.
7.   Take a hike and observe gall formations. Draw some. In February bring galls inside, place in screen cages, and see what emerges.
8.   Visit a beekeeper and watch a bee on a flower.
9.   Keep track of which insects are attracted to certain flowers. Can you find color, smell, or shape differences?
10.   Describe the parts of an insect without telling what you are describing and have the students draw a picture of the "critter."

Warning: Beware of overemphasis on the killing of insects. Let people enjoy the insects in nature so that they can appreciate the role that they play, rather than thinking of them as dead specimens.

Moths and Butterflies

Of all the insects that we encounter, the bird-like butterflies are probably the most impressive because of their color and passive behavior. Lepidoptera is also the easiest family to identify.

Butterflies and moths are easy to observe and they make excellent study subjects. Do not over-collect them, but a few species can be taken for study. You should consider studying their life cycles as well as categorizing and naming them.

Questions for Study and Discussion

1.   What is the difference between moths and butterflies?
2.   What are the stages of metamorphosis?
3.   What means of protection are used by butterflies?

Projects

1. Make butterfly nets.
2. Collect, identify, and release butterflies.
3. Hunt for butterfly eggs, pupae, and cocoons.
4. Build cages and raise butterflies.
5. Make both day and night collections. Use a white light reflected off of a white sheet for night collecting.
6. Observe one type of butterfly and make a list of all species of plant that it visits. Watch for egg laying.
7. Make a bulletin board showing food species for butterfly and larvae.
8. Mix stale beer, ripe banana, and sugar. Coat trees with it to attract moths.
9. Find out if someone in the area is banding butterflies and see if you can work with them.
10. Find butterflies in art and design. Include music and drama.

ECOLOGY

The study of individual groups of plants and animals is only a beginning in nature study. The most important lessons we can provide are understandings of the interrelationships that exist: the life cycles. A habitat is an area that meets the requirements for life of any one species. Many habitats are present in any area, but the variety and number are usually limited by the combination of plants. Factors that influence the plant communities are water, soil, and sunlight. Large plant communities that characterize a region are called biomes.

Activities

1. Visit different areas and compare them.
2. Look for small plant communities within an area. Discuss why differences can exist within such a small area.
3. Make a line transect or a hoop transect.
4. Find and list plants and animals that exist in more than one community and discuss specializations and adaptations.
5. Build a terrarium representing one of the communities and discuss its needs.
6. Discuss and chart cycles: food webs, nitrogen, carbon, water, and oxygen.
7. Put caterpillars in cages with plants and see if they eat any plant or have a preference for one type.

8. Grow plants in various amounts of sunshine and water and see how tolerant they are to different conditions.

9. Adopt a stream or a park and make its environmental health your class concern.

Plant Communities Study. The information gathered from the following questions and suggested actions will aid in the study of plant communities.

What kind of habitat is the particular area of study?

What plants have you observed?

How tall were the plants?

Draw one of the plants.

What is the most abundant plant?

List animal signs.

Was the area wet or dry?

What did you like about this place?

What are the most abundant colors?

Do any colors stand out?

Describe the sounds you hear.

What odors are present?

Is the water clear, murky, moving, or standing?

How does this plant community differ from the surrounding area?

Draw a food web showing possible relationships in this plant community.

Another possible approach to outdoor education is the use of classroom disciplines as the study objectives. The following ideas are samples for non-science subjects.

Arithmetic

1. Measure the following: a board foot; age of tree through ring count; circumference and diameter of trees; surface area for map making, scale drawing or models; dimensions of buildings; pacing distance; distances between buildings, trees. Also, make biltmore sticks and hypsometers.

2. Estimate the following: percent of slope; height of tree; time of day; distance away from lightning; distance hiked or canoed; width of a river; how many trees on the school grounds; number of board feet in a log; speed of water flow and gallons of flow per second; bird populations at feeders.

Outdoor Activities **3.**   Average the following: temperature readings; barometric readings; precipitation.

4.   Other possible projects are to estimate and measure the height of trees through the measurement of shadows; to find the amount and cost of gravel for a roadbed; to plan amounts and costs of food for cook-outs; to plot a graph of the weather; to hike with a compass; to operate a stop watch to determine speed of walking; to pace distances in hiking; to stake out an area of ground; to cut and pile a cord of fireplace wood; to mark out a garden plot; to find the cost for seeding or resodding a plot; to count the average number of trees in an acre.

Language Arts

1. Learn folklore.
2. Keep field notes in areas of special interest.
3. Use the library for research reading on bird species at a feeder.
4. Label and identify specimens.
5. Have verbal discussions or debates on environmental issues.
6. Play and lead games.
7. Write poems, diaries, logs, newspapers, stories, songs, plays, essays.
8. Learn the communication techniques of wolves and birds.
9. Have group discussions in planning and evaluating program activities.
10. Learn new words obtained from nature and conversation.
11. Listen for sounds in nature.
12. Write and put on a puppet play.
13. Do a dramatization of animals (mammals, insects, birds, reptiles, and amphibians).
14. Imitate animal sounds.
15. Communicate without words.

Social Studies

1. Learn to make Indian tools and materials.
2. Construct a pioneer building and household articles.
3. Make a community study.
4. Visit local spots of historical interest.

Outdoor Activities

5. Do handicrafts out of natural materials.
6. Visit a cemetery.
7. Visit a junkyard.
8. What are the community's recreational demands and what kinds of facilities are needed to meet those demands?
9. Learn about renewable and non-renewable natural resources.
10. Learn about depletion of natural resources.
11. Learn about the restoration of natural resources.
12. Learn how the government helps develop, control, and protect natural resources.
13. Recreate an historic event from your area.
14. Interview senior citizens.

Health and Physical Education

1. Plan healthful meals.
2. Write safety rules for camping and camp gear.
3. Learn how to purify water.
4. Make a manual of first aid for expeditions.
5. Plan clothing lists for winter and summer camping trips.
6. Plan exercise routines to get into shape for biking, skiing, backpacking.
7. Do casting and angling (bait and fly).
8. Practice archery.
9. Practice marksmanship.
10. Play games.
11. Enjoy winter sports (ice fishing, skiing, making and using snowshoes).
12. Enjoy swimming, boating, canoeing, and sailing.
13. Plan trails for hiking.
14. Plan and carry out an expedition.
15. Go fishing.

Arts, Crafts, and Music

1. Make game equipment.
2. Make simple camp furniture.
3. Sketch, draw, color and/or paint natural scenes.

4. Do clay work using natural clays; collect them yourself.
5. Weave grasses, barks, reeds.
6. Do nature photography.
7. Do tree fungus carving.
8. Compose songs about nature.
9. Listen to night sounds and compare with recordings.
10. Imitate bird calls.
11. Paint, photograph, or draw the same scene in different seasons or weather conditions.
12. Make and play primitive instruments.
13. Learn folk songs and their origins and meanings.

Six

Writing Your Own Units

The inevitable mark of wisdom is to see the miraculous in the common.

RALPH WALDO EMERSON

Activities are the building blocks to knowledge. Through activities, the students come to understand their environment and develop a personal philosophy. Activities are constructed around concepts, measured in learner outcomes, and grouped into study units. The creators of units must explore the intricacies of a particular study site or subject and explore the possibilities with their senses and physical presence.

Environmental education is the study of our relationship to the environment and its natural cycles. The subject matter falls into five categories.

1. The natural environment
2. The artificial environment
3. The interaction between the artificial and natural environments
4. The consequences of the interactions
5. Judgment or values

As an example, let us choose to study a rock wall. In our initial observations we conclude that the rocks are in this area as part of a natural environment, but actually, the fact of the wall's placement there makes this an arbitrary artificial environment. Over the years the components of the natural eco-systems have added new ingredients to the wall and have naturalized it. As a consequence, many animals have found new homes, and plants have been able to establish themselves. These plants and animals could not exist in either the field or woods that are adjacent to the wall. In fact, the wall has helped to maintain the integrity of both environments by limiting the root suckers that would move the forest into the field.

A value judgment for this situation would be required to decide whether to remove or leave the rock wall in order to have a natural area. Is there a point at which the "unnatural" becomes "natural"? Where would the animals and plant colonizers go if the wall were removed? Are either of the last two questions pertinent to the decision?

RESOURCE INVENTORY

The preparation of a study unit begins with an inventory of the ingredients of the area to be studied. In broad terms the ingredients are:

1. meteorological conditions
2. geology
3. flora
4. fauna (excluding people)
5. human history

All places on Earth are a combination of meteorological and geological forces which combine to form the life support systems (climate) of an area. Based on the interaction of these two systems the biological process emerges in steps. The plants create the food source that allows animals to survive, and the sum of the first four groups determines the conditions of human interaction.

A partial inventory of our rock wall conditions might look like this:

Meteorological Conditions

1. The wind changes direction and speeds from top to bottom and from side to side on the wall
2. Wet and dry places

Plant life may be inconspicuous and curious.

3. Speed of growth
4. Size of plants
5. Does humidity vary along the wall?
6. How much impact does solar energy have on or in the wall?
7. Where does the rain go that hits the top rocks?
8. Where is it coldest? Where is it warmest?
9. What is the wall like in the different seasons?

Geological Conditions

1. What kinds of rocks make up the wall?
2. What holds them together?
3. Where did the rocks come from?
4. Is there soil on the rocks? Where did it come from?
5. How many rocks are in the wall?
6. How much does the rock wall weigh? What is its volume?
7. Is the rock wall growing? Is it shrinking?
8. What causes the rocks to move?

Flora

1. Locations for plant growth
2. Lichens
3. Mosses
4. Flowering plants
5. Dead plants
6. Nutrients
7. Decomposition
8. Biomass
9. Wild foods and herbs
10. Speed of growth
11. Size of plants
12. Why do plants grow better on one portion of the wall than on another?

Fauna

1. Snakes
2. Chipmunks
3. Tracks
4. Birds
5. Nests
6. Cavities
7. Homes
8. Insects

Human History

1. Hours of labor
2. Why?
3. How?
4. When?
5. Who?
6. Signs of past humans
7. Signs of current humans
8. Rock wall in literature and art

Brainstorm. Now that you have categorized your subject, you should start to brainstorm about everything that could be done to study each component. The rule in brainstorming is to put down your wildest idea and your most conservative one, and then fill in the gaps in between. Be outlandish first and expand your mind to include the ridiculous. The most dangerous tendency is to put together a sequence of activities immediately. If you do, there are some exciting and innovative thoughts that will never surface.

Brainstorming ideas for the rock wall might include trying to live on the wall for a week, watching a plant grow to maturity, and finding the textures, the colors, the shapes, and the designs in the wall. Activities might include photography, crayon drawings, or even constructing a new wall just like the old one. You could move every rock to count them or you could put miniature rain gauges into little cracks and nooks.

When you have written down all the ideas you can think of, take a break and let your mind rest. Do something different, think about something else, until you are refreshed. Then go back to your list and read over all of the ideas you have put down.

Objectives. Determine the objectives for your study. In the following study for the rock wall, we have used the learner outcome from Chapter 3, which says, "Describe humans as an integral part of the natural world, influenced by natural processes." Emphasis is on the concept "niche" and on the skills of reasoning and inference based on the data collected.

Organize Ideas. Eliminate the impossible activities on your list of ideas and then list the remaining ideas on a sheet of paper with the following nine evaluative columns. To save time, review the first three columns for all of the ideas first, crossing out any activities that do not have a check in all three of these columns. Then go on with the rest of the evaluations.

1.   Time: Can the activity be done within the given time frame?
2.   Objectives: Will the activity add to the overall goals that have been set?
3.   Age group: Is the activity appropriate for the target age group?
4.   Inside/Outside: Put an "I" or "O" in this column, depending on where the activity is best done. If it can be done equally well in both places, use a "B".
5.   Approaches: Use a letter to indicate which of these techniques describes the approach that an individual activity takes: (a) Data collecting (investigation), (b) Alteration of the environment, (c) Documentary research (historical), (d) Sensory experience, (e) Futurism-projection, (f) Sociological (interview, current history),

(g) Economics, (h) Recreation, (i) Observation, (j) Visual recording (mapping, photography, art).

6. Presentation: Use a letter that corresponds with the way you think each part of the remaining activity package will be presented. (a) Lecture and observation (b) Lecture and experiment (c) Directed discussion (d) Directed experimentation/discovery (e) Open-ended discovery (unknown ending) (f) Chaos: no direction, no expectation, see what happens.

7. Sequence: Indicate the order in which the remaining activities should be done. Take into consideration the skills and backgrounds that are needed and whether some of the activities might prepare a student for later studies.

8. Parallel activity: Check activities that can be done by part of the group, thereby freeing the remainder of the group to do other studies. This type of activity gives students responsibility and freedom, and the accumulation of information from the different groups expands the scope of the class activity.

9. Retain: Look at the time your remaining activities take. Eliminate redundancy, weakness, and parts that demand more time than they deserve in relation to the contribution the activity makes to the

The wall is a unique garden.

whole. Cross out those eliminated, but only lightly, because they might be useful at another time or as alternate ideas. Try to mix approaches and presentations.

Finishing Touches. When your unit is written up, retain an outline format. This is a clean, quick way of presenting the necessary information, the scope of its contents, and the flow from activity to activity. The outline leaves room for the individual instructors to put in their own notes and create their own ideas.

The last item in writing up your own study unit is the evaluation. Make it a part of the learning experience through an activity which summarizes the knowledge that is acquired or one which uses the knowledge gained and applies it to a new situation. Tests are a standard evaluation method, but essays, photographs, drawings, journals, discussions, and performance are also means of measurement.

The following activity is a sample rock wall unit in its finished form.

I. ROCK WALL STUDY—How does a rock wall fit into the environment?
   A. Goals
      1. Interpretation of natural clues
      2. Understanding how nature may adopt an artificial object
      3. Understanding habitat and niche
   B. Grades
      1. 4–6
   C. Lesson In-class
      1. Read Frost's poem "The Mending Wall." Students should write meaning.
      2. Discussion of rock walls
         a. Where are they found?
         b. What are some of the possible reasons for their creation?
         c. When was it made?
         d. Who made it? Why?
         e. What is it made of?
         f. Where did the materials come from?
   D. Interpretation
      1. Look at map of rock wall's location on study property.
         a. Where is it located?
         b. Why is it located there?

E. Field Investigations (Can be divided and done simulta-
neously.)
1. Observation
   a. What is it made of?
   b. What sizes, colors, shapes?
2. Investigation and recording
   a. How big is it? Guess the length, then measure.
   b. How much does it weigh? Sampling.
   c. What direction does it go?
   d. What are the angles of its slope?
3. Define micro-habitats
   a. Discussion
   b. Investigate conditions
      (1) Where is moisture most? Least?
      (2) Measure temperature variations.
   c. Investigate and record plant and animal life and
      signs.
      (1) Types of plants and where located.
      (2) Types of animals and where located.
      (3) Are they the same or different than the sur-
          rounding area?
      (4) Are the same plants and animals all over the
          entire rock wall, or do they seem to be in small
          but similar areas (niche) on the rock wall?
      (5) Make up a food web that might exist entirely
          on the rock wall and one that might be only
          partially on the wall and with the surrounding
          area.
4. Dynamics: Does it change? (Observation and interpretation)
   a. How would this fence have looked when it was first
      made?
   b. Is the rock wall changing? Growing or shrinking?
   c. Do the rocks move? In what possible ways? (wind,
      frost heave, ice, animals, plant roots)
   d. What has been added to the wall besides animals
      and plants? (sediment, dust, pollen, seeds, litter)
   e. How will the wall eventually look?

F. Follow-up
1. Is a rock wall natural when it is made? Will it ever be
   natural?
2. Draw a picture of the rock wall as you remember it and
   as you think it will look 500 years from now.

G. Review Objectives
   1. Students should understand that everything affects and is affected by nature.
   2. Understand the concepts of niche, habitat, ecotone.
   3. Develop ability to reason and make inferences with collected data and observations.
       a. Understand change
       b. Apply classroom skills to the outdoor environment
H. Evaluation
   1. Read Frost's poem and react to it.
   2. Could man live entirely on the rock wall? Write an essay.
   3. Have students find other artificial objects that are now deserted and make a photo essay. Discuss if they are as easily assimilated in the natural environment as a rock wall.
I. Alternate Activity
   1. Make a rock wall out of schoolyard stones in a terrarium.

Content Analysis.   After your unit is written, scrutinize it one more time. Take each experience or skill and ask why you have included it. Then ask what the teacher should do to prepare for each part. Table 6.1 is an analysis of the rock wall study.

Evaluate your finished work using the evaluating criteria used by the Western Pennsylvania Conservancy in their evaluations of environmental education curriculum materials.

1. They should be involvement-oriented.
2. They should emphasize ethical behavior.
3. They should be interdisciplinary.
4. They should be flexible.

Phyllis Gross and Esther Railton in *Teaching Science In An Outdoor Environment,* have an even longer check list of pertinent questions which they apply to an education program. How does your material score on this list?

1.   Science education today: Are the students experiencing, discovering, thinking? Are you capitalizing on the "wonder" syndrome?
2.   Learning: Are you alert to changes in behavior in the three domains of instructional objectives?
3.   The learner: Are provisions made for individual differences in

Table 6.1. Analysis of Rock Wall Study

Experience/Skill	Why?	Teacher Preparation
Reading poem	Develop ability to understand how others may feel about an object and see how an inanimate object might evoke feelings	Review poem
Discussion	Determine students' familiarity with subject. Establish common ground for future study. Develop awareness of varying perceptions of common object.	Investigate prevalence of rock walls, as well as rock piles in the area. Where and why? Determine an area to be studied and get permission to use it. Arrange permission slips for students, transportation and school administration permission.
Interpretation and map	Develop skills for use of a map. Develop skills of deduction.	Make or acquire the map.
Observation, investigation and recording	Application of basic math to problem solving. Develop skill to gather data for use in future problem solving.	Familiarity with compass and sampling techniques.
Micro habitat investigation and recording	Develop understanding of basic needs of life.	Prepare recording procedure. Be familiar with existing life. Secure necessary equipment.
Dynamics	Develop understanding of change as a natural process. Develop ability to analyze data which has been collected. Make inferences.	Familiarity with succession
Follow-up	Develop ability to recall concepts and images	Materials
Relate outdoor experience to the classroom.	Allows teacher to observe impact and effectiveness of study.	
Evaluation	Extension of study to new ideas.	Materials

intellectual development? Do students have ample opportunity for moving to the next stage of development?

4.   Objectives: Are objectives stated in behavioral (testable) terms? Do students have the opportunity to assist in determining goals? Are "facts" the end goal or are they used as a tool for more intellectual activities? Do "tests" include a wide variety of observable student behaviors?

5. Process and content: May students use their own initiative in solving problems? Are students learning to use appropriate intellectual skills? Do the students have an opportunity to fit whatever knowledge they have gained into a "big idea" (conceptual system)?

6. Is creativity being encouraged?

At this stage the study unit needs the infusion of life and personality. It needs the excitement of involvement, a class, the outdoors, and an enthusiastic teacher.

Seven

Your Local Nature Center

Climb the mountains and get their good tidings. Nature's peace will flow into you as sunshine flows into trees. The winds will blow their own freshness into you, and the storms their energy, while cares will drop off like autumn leaves.

JOHN MUIR

Nature centers are sanctuaries for plants and animals, and for the people who love them. They are oases of solitude and learning. The proper way to use a nature center is to use it often. Teachers should attend the classes that are offered, walk the trails, and attend the public programs.

Teachers should also inform their students about programs at the centers and encourage them to attend with family and friends. This is a place to build acquaintances and to develop a love for the outdoors. Use the rules in Chapter 1 to set up your visit and then take advantage of every moment that your class is outdoors.

BECOMING INVOLVED WITH A NATURE CENTER

Wood Lake Nature Center, Richfield, Minnesota, uses the following procedure for teacher registration.

Teachers call Wood Lake to arrange a field trip on one day per season. For example, fall tour registration day is September 8th. We will not take reservations before then as the naturalist schedule usually is not concrete before that date. At the time of the call, we reserve a date and time for a tour and obtain their name, address, phone number, school or group name, number of students coming and the age of the students. We mark these into our Log Book and then a confirmation sheet and field activity summary sheet are sent out to the teacher. Once they have looked over the options they call back and talk to the naturalist(s) taking their group to select a unit. After a choice has been made the teachers are sent a "Pre/Post Activity" set corresponding to their unit. This packet is sent out in enough time for the teacher to have the students go over the materials. It has been observed in the past to be most helpful for the students to have some idea of what to expect at Wood Lake during their field trip. The naturalists find it makes the trip easier, with less repetition of facts, if the class has done the "homework" relating to the unit. For the teachers, many seem to appreciate this extra information to be done back in the classroom as this helps tie the field experience in with what they did prior to the visit.

The following section contains a summary of the summer field activities at Wood Lake Nature Center.

Dear Teacher or Leader:

Here is a selection of activities you can do at Wood Lake this summer. Please call us with the activity you want to do so the naturalists will be able to prepare for your visit.

See you in the marsh!

THE STAFF OF WOOD LAKE

Preschool—Kindergarten

Critter Walk Children use their senses to explore the friendly outdoors.

Animal Coloration Children find animal skins placed outside and discover how color is useful as adaptation. Children can also camouflage themselves and play animal hide and seek. Post-activity slide show.

Like and Different Children practice spotting similarities and differences in tracks, animals, trees, shapes, etc.

Toes in the Marsh A first look at the marsh as an exciting place to visit.

```
Wood Lake Nature Center
735 Lake Shore Drive
Richfield, Minnesota  55423

Your group of _____ is now scheduled to work with _____
                                              .
naturalist(s) on:_____, from_____.
                   (date)            (time)
Each naturalist will work with a maximum of 15 people.

Your naturalist will be:_____.


To give you an idea of what we can do here, we have enclosed a
summary sheet with some of our favorite field study units that work
best for this season.  Look through the list and select an activity
to do with your group.  Then call your naturalist and let him or her
know your choice.  He or she would be happy to help you with your
choice.

PLEASE BRING AT LEAST ONE ADULT FOR EVERY 15 STUDENTS

Before your field trip...

Please familiarize your group with the use of the nature center

as a place to...
                    come,
                     listen,
                       and wonder,

but  NOT to pick plants, harass or feed the animals, or go off the

trails.

Our museum has touch and see tables where you are welcome to pick up
and examine various objects.  PLEASE limit touching to those exhibits
only.

Thank you for your cooperation--see you soon and REMEMBER TO CALL
YOUR NATURALIST TODAY!

Note:  To arrange a tour for your group for the _____ season,

please call on:_____.
                 (date)
```

First and Second Grade

Colors, Shapes and Textures Children use rainbow cards and a magic viewer to find colors and shapes outside. Textures are impressed on clay.

The World of Little Children use magnifying glasses to get a close look at tiny things along the trail. Especially interesting things can be brought to the building and "blown up" with our microscope projector so everyone can see them.

Leaf Prints Children find leaves, match them up with the parent plants, and make ink prints to take home.

121

Cold Blooded "Critters" Who's afraid of a cold blooded "critter"?

We look at fish, worms, turtles and snakes indoors as well as out. If desired, children can watch the snake eat a "snack."

Worm Cookies For the adventurous group! We will dig up worms, study their life cycle and then make and eat worm cookies if the group desires. (We are *not* kidding!)

Third and Fourth Grade

Whistles and Squawkers Learn to make old-fashioned musical toys from natural materials you find on the trail.

Stickbread Students grind corn and wild seeds by hand, then build a fire and cook their stickbread over the coals.

Pond Study Children dip their cups into the "magic" water and come up with bugs and whirligigs and many-legged creatures. An introduction to the marsh.

Tracks and Homes of Animals Students find signs of animal activity, then preserve tracks with plaster of paris so they can be taken home.

Summer Art After exploring the area, children create a work of wonder to take home.

Minibeasts Using nets and magnifying boxes, students go on a minibeast scavenger hunt to find and observe insects and other small animals.

Cave Walk Something else for the adventurous groups! We will explore the urban caves called storm sewers to see what they are for and what is in them.

Fifth and Sixth Grade

Butterfly Banding How do you band a butterfly? Put an iron ring on its foot? Come and find out!

Stickbread Students grind corn and wild seeds by hand, then build a fire and cook their stickbread over the coals.

Handmade Paper Paper you make yourself from bark, cattail fluff and other natural materials is the most beautiful paper in the world. There may be time to make your own ink.

Wild Edible Plants Students differentiate between common plant families, then find, examine, and taste samples of wild edible plants. Follow-up done at home or school.

Marooned Students find themselves marooned in the woods, prairie, or marsh, and try to devise a way of life based on the natural resources of their area. Groups meet later to compare cultures. Social studies, science, or even dramatics can be emphasized.

Advanced Pond Study Students use individualized project cards to explore and compare three natural communities: the woods, the marsh, and the prairie.

Minibeasts Using nets and magnifying boxes, students go on a minibeast scavenger hunt to find and observe insects and other small animals.

Hot Air Balloon Make and launch a small, unmanned hot air balloon.

Orienteering Try our new trails! Students follow their map and compass to different locations throughout the entire Wood Lake area. You can travel fast or slow, but whoever reaches the most locations and answers the most questions correctly will be the winner!

Junior and Senior High

Many of these units can be adapted to suit your group's particular needs. We especially recommend the fifth and sixth grade units.

When you have completed registration, the center would forward a description of the field activity and pre and post activity suggestions.

WHAT TO WEAR

Dressing adequately for weather conditions is a must. Students often find the experience at a nature center a negative one if they are very cold or wet. The day before the trip, listen to the weather forecast for the next day's temperatures, wind speed, and chance of rain. Plan accordingly. It is often cooler and more windy in park or wilderness areas than in the city.

Each winter one of the biggest problems is cold and numb feet. Girls especially have this problem, because "fashion" boots are usually too thin and too tight. They are made for looks, not warmth. Boys get cold feet too, if their feet are not dressed just right. You can't have much fun—or learn anything—if your feet are freezing. Frostbite can be a real danger! To dress your feet for winter you need:

1.   room enough to wiggle your toes. Avoid packing your boots so full of socks you can't move your toes. This will cut off the circulation of warm blood to your feet. You may wish to wear boots a size too large

to allow enough room for your feet. Wear two pairs of socks and allow air space, which acts as insulation.

2.   layers, because one pair of socks (except in snowmobile boots) is not enough. Most boots are thin rubber or plastic and the cold comes right through. So be sure to wear two pairs of socks or snowmobile boots with felt liner.

3.   warm socks, wool or insulated. Cotton socks are too thin. Wool is much better: it traps more air, which acts as insulation. Wool also absorbs sweat better.

4.   dry feet. Avoid wearing boots which are already wet inside. If your boots have a hole in them, or are wet from yesterday, put a plastic bag (like a bread bag) outside your socks before putting on your boots.

The teacher or leader's role at the nature center is important. Here are some guidelines that will help you make the best of your experience. Be enthusiastic. The trip should not be hurried; take your time and help students enjoy what they do. Activities should not lag. Be quick to direct students' attention to something new if you feel interest waning. Be prepared for the unexpected. Take the time to investigate a different plant, animal, or unusual rock.

Adjust the speed of walking and distance to the age group.

Children at the pre-school level should prepare for abstract thinking with a concrete experience. This is why it is necessary for the children to make use of the five senses. They should see, smell, hear, feel, and taste the different things outside on a very limited level, not just be told about it.

Children learn from you by example more than by statement. For example, your positive concern for the area will impress them with a need for taking care, so you too should "touch but don't take" and "put everything back." Be willing to do anything you ask of the children. If you cannot hide your own fears at least admit to them.

Look for opportunities to answer questions from children with another question or a statement that will make them look more closely at an object. A direct answer without a directed observation usually closes the discussion and no more learning (observing) will take place.

Quarry Hill is the only nature center in the Rochester, Minnesota area, and it is part of the school district. The director, Harry Buck, outlined the expectations that are associated with his center:

When we began eight years ago, we had visions of training all 500 elementary teachers to lead or at least help with the leading of their activities at Quarry Hill. After two years of in-service classes, etc., we came to the conclusion that there was no way that we could train that many teachers in a program which was undergoing constant change and expansion. In our system, teachers were required to take in-service classes in handwriting, math, science, drug abuse, and human relations, plus other voluntary classes. We did not feel that we could add another layer. We do expect the teacher to participate, however. Each of our activities has pre-visit material to prepare them for the visit and post-visit material which summarizes/analyzes the data collected and observed. We must rely on the teacher to provide this introduction and follow-up. We have, on occasion, when time permits, gone back to the classroom to conduct the follow-up study. This serves a two-fold purpose; it allows us to see how effective our device is and allows us to demonstrate to the teacher how the follow-up might be conducted. This is particularly helpful for new teachers and/or those who feel unsure about what they have done and what their role is in the follow-up.

Let me give a couple of examples of what we expect a teacher to do:

Item 1: Activity on topographic mapping. Teacher begins with a two week SAPA unit on contour maps. From the Nature Center comes a topographic model of the city of Rochester, cut from

A naturalist determines his own style, and that gives a program its strength and uniqueness. Dennis Olson has become "critterman" and has used that identity to reach many groups.

styrofoam on the 100 ft. contour interval. Students are asked to locate certain geographic or man-made features on the model. They then are given the problem which says, if you were standing at spot X on the model, would you be able to see the features identified? This is all done before the visit and is teacher-directed.

During their visit to the Nature Center, the students are given directions on how to make a simple topographic map and they do it under the direction of the Nature Center staff. As a second part of the activity, they walk to the spot marked X on their model and actually determine whether or not they can see the identified place or object.

As a take-home activity to be administered by the teacher, we send a sheet showing topographic map symbols, a simple topographic map, and a set of questions about the map. We also send a set of five USGS topographic maps of Rochester, Minnesota; Ely, Minnesota; Ennis, Montana; Aransas, Texas; and Wabasha, Minnesota; along with questions about each map which will require a good basic understanding of topographic maps. We have yet to find a student who does *not* like to work with topographic maps, nor have we found a teacher who did not use their follow-up material.

Necessary information for the teacher (ex., answer keys, set-up suggestions, and suggested procedures) are included with each packet. Although the teachers generally have never been exposed to topographic maps, enough information is provided with the pre and post-visits to make them more knowledgeable than their students (or experts).

Item 2: An activity on succession in which the students look at our quarry to see what has happened since the quarrying activity stopped and then make a prediction on how the quarry will look after fifty years. The pre-visit material consists of a set of large pictures (commercially prepared) showing the stages of succession along with printed labels (prepared by us) which can become an excellent bulletin board display in the classroom. Also included is a single sheet of information for teachers, which explains succession using the proper vocabulary. These things are done by the teacher before the visit.

During the visit, students measure the physical factors both inside and outside of the quarry. They find temperature, humidity, wind velocity, light penetration, etc. They also measure soil depth. The biotic factors are measured with a line transect (forty meters) and measuring and identifying all the trees in that area. All of this information is recorded on a data sheet along with observations of animal evidence which might have an effect on succession. This part of the activity is led by the Nature Center staff with help from the teachers involved. When classes return to school, their task is to analyze the data and make a prediction of how the quarry will look after fifty years of succession. This may take the form of a written narrative or a drawing of the landscape.

In order that gratification be more instant than fifty years down the road, we have prepared a filmstrip which shows stages of succession in quarries of various ages in southeastern Minnesota. We happen to have a fifty year old quarry within three miles of our quarry for easy comparison. This analysis, prediction, and filmstrip, are carried out by the teacher in the classroom.

We feel that the student experience is generally of better quality if we use staff and/or volunteers to carry out the actual visit. We do, however, expect and insist that teachers accompany their groups while doing the activities at the Nature Center. We purposely do not have a coffee pot because that becomes more important than the task-at-hand with some teachers.

Many urban nature centers limit visits to an hour and a half in length and then spend up to half of that time indoors, because going outside right away presents too many "distractions". If those distractions were accepted as regular events and part of the learning experience, it might get people outside longer with greater impact—and that is the purpose of outdoor education.

Work around obstacles and prepare your class so that they can be involved every minute. This means that you must know what you want to do on your field trip and what you want to stress. Tell the naturalist what you are studying in the classroom and ask for suggestions regarding activities that can be done at the nature center to reinforce the classroom learning.

Set times that are advantageous to the class and to the study. Maximize the transportation cost by planning all day studies and, if the naturalist cannot be with you for that length of time, see if the Center can suggest activities for you to do for the remainder of your visit. Perhaps the naturalist can start you out and then do a wrap-up with your group before you return to the school. Volunteers may be able to assist your group during the time that the naturalist is with another group.

Plan to use bus time for a purpose. Set up bus observation studies or use travel time for lecture. The bus is moving on school time and it is during this time that students can lose sight of the day's purpose. Ideas that could be used on bus trips include:

Preserve or Environmental Study Site Data Form

Name:

County: Town: State:

Coordinates of approximate center:

_____latitude   _____longitude

Name and address of person filling out form:

_____

_____

Checklist:

Maps

___location   ___vegetation

___topographic with boundaries   ___aquatic features

___special natural features   ___historical features

___soils   ___improvements

Other

___climatic information   ___reference studies

___aerial photos   ___references and publications

___lists of animal and plant   ___deed
    species

___research studies

Geological

___gorges   ___natural sand, beach, dune

___distinctive mountain features ___ancient beach

___cliffs, bluffs, rims   ___islands

___rock outcrops: natural   ___fossil evidence

___rock outcrops: manmade   ___cave formations

___volcanic evidence   ___sinkholes or karst

___glacial features   ___other

Name of other:_____

Hydrological

___whitewater stretches   ___swamps

___waterfalls   ___estuaries

___natural springs   ___reversing falls

___marshes   ___stream or river with
                                      anadromous fish
___bogs
                                  ___other

Name of other:_____

Scientific, Archeological, Cultural, and Historical
___site of previous scientific   ___historical buildings
   research
                                        ___historical sites
___native campsites, villages, etc.   ___other

___native artifacts

Name of other:_____

Describe the outstanding geological, hydrological, scientific,
archaeological, cultural, and historical features. Take the
feature name from the checklist.

Feature:_____   Description:_____
_____
Feature:_____   Description:_____
_____

1. Road Kills: number and kind per unit of distance. Are they an indication of a specific animal's habitat in the area you are traveling?

2. How long are the white, interrupted lines that are in the middle of the highway? Try to devise a way to calculate this while the bus is moving.

3. Influences of automobiles: (a) Number of signs dealing with the auto industry, (b) Number of cars, kinds, variety of licenses, (c) Number of people in vehicles you meet and pass. Is car pooling being used? Should it be?

4. Census of easily recognized birds.

5. Think metric! What is your speed in kilometers? What is the distance in kilometers?

6. Attempt to analyze density of people (mailbox counts) and proximity to towns, or the various types of stores and services along the highway.

7. Billboards: types, frequency, size, topics. Aesthetics. Why are they there? Are they necessary?

8. Color of barns, houses, and other buildings. How do colors blend in with the environment?

9. Bullet holes in signs. Graffiti. Do you respect people who do damage like this?

10. Telephone and electric poles. Calculate distance and incidence.

11. Trucks, pickups, cars, trailers, campers, and boats that are met as you travel. Can you tell where they are going? Are

there enough wild places to allow all the people in the United States to visit them at the same time?

The teacher often expends so much effort in the classroom as instructor, disciplinarian and parent, that an outsider is needed periodically to infuse a new atmosphere into the learning experience. The naturalist at a nature center can add a new voice, approach, mannerisms and ideas. Groups can be divided into smaller units and the teacher can help or become the assistant. A good naturalist should be able to give additional background to the teacher.

Know the trails at the center you are visiting and learn what displays and equipment are available before your visit. Be prepared for all weather conditions and leave students behind who are not prepared with the proper clothing, or the proper mental attitude. Do not let them ruin your outing, and make sure that everyone knows that they are expected to learn from the session, perhaps even be tested on it.

A successful outing to a nature center is the culmination of the talents of the naturalists, teacher, and class, as well as the wise use of the center's land and facilities.

Eight

Workshops for Teachers

The imagination of man brings him close to the doorway of the infinite, which encompasses all. I often think of early man with his first nebulous dream at the very threshold of his rise, stirred by vague and frightening fears of the unknown.

SIGURD OLSON

It is easy to ask, even to demand, that teachers use the outdoor classroom and that they teach environmental education, but what do you ask them to give up? New programs demand preparation and study time and should not take away from the basic skills a student must receive. So what do you tell a class of teachers? Integrate. That is the key to environmental education. The teacher need not add a subject, but need only change an emphasis.

A workshop for teachers should demonstrate the materials which should be kept at a minimum, have simple instructions, and offer activities that can be duplicated without hours of preparation. A workshop should simplify the teacher's job.

In 1971 the National Education Association (NEA) set up guidelines for environmental study area workshops. These guidelines, which are still appropriate, began with the following instructional strategies:

1. The learner learns best when he is actively engaged in what is being taught.

2. The learner learns best when he is using all his senses.
3. Each learner has a unique way of processing information and experience.
4. The learner learns something new in relation to something he already knows.
5. The learner learns what seems important to him—what he feels a need to learn.
6. Discovering for oneself generates a sense of excitement and satisfaction that reinforces learning.

To these strategies might be added a seventh: the learner attends a workshop to gain immediately useful knowledge, not to gain an additional workload of further research and reading.

The mechanics of a workshop should strive to set a quick pace that keeps everyone alert: vary the presentation to prevent lulls; have students change place and attitude periodically; have enough breaks for meals, snacks, toilet use, or rest; and reflect the learner assumptions.

Workshops require planning and that requires a dedicated committee that understands what planning is. The Minnesota Environmental Science Foundation gives planning the following definition:

1. Planning is not forecasting, in fact, it is needed because we cannot forecast.
2. Planning does not deal with future decisions, but the future implications of the present decision.
3. Planning is not an attempt to eliminate risk, but to minimize.
4. It is a continuous process of systematic decision making, systematic efforts to carry out decisions, and a systematic measurement of feedback.

A workshop must have a staff that can be respected by the participants and appropriate handouts to supplement the discussions and activities. The NEA has developed the following process of workshop design:

1. Determining goals and deriving specific objectives.
2. Brainstorming for activities that support learning and are in line with the specific objectives.
3. Determining limiting factors.
4. Selecting the most appropriate activities.

5. Sequencing the activities.
6. Determining support systems needed to conduct the workshop (materials and people).
7. Developing a workshop schedule.

To set workshop goals and objectives the committee should begin with a simple exercise in which each person lists what they perceive as the mission of the workshop and four objectives that will help the workshop achieve that goal. These lists can then be collected, synthesized, and used as the basis of discussion and decision.

To determine the limiting factors, begin two lists. Have half of your group list all of the factors that could make a workshop a grand success, and have the other half list all the possible problems that could cause the workshop to fail.

Exchange the lists and have the groups score each item as "highly probable," "possible," or "unlikely," and then list a solution to the problem or conditions which would be necessary for the success factor to happen.

Combine the two lists and discuss the results. Are there any new factors that should be added to either list? Is assistance required from new people or organizations? Who is responsible for any follow-up to these areas?

To select the proper activities to include in the workshop, list each activity on a sheet of paper that has the following categories.

1. Activity
2. Time needed
3. Importance of activity to overall goal
4. What percentage of target audience will benefit from it?
5. Is there a cost for materials for this activity?

The workshop time, audience, and goal will all be factors in your decision and this chart should help the decision process.

The plan should have some back up ideas: contingency plans and alternatives for participants where topics become specialized in appeal. Be flexible enough to reorder the workshop if it shows signs of failing.

If college credits are an important inducement, work with a college which is used to doing in-service types of programs. Tell them what you are planning to do and request that credits be given. Tell them specifically what you want from them: personnel, students, advertising, credits.

Colleges usually want their staff involved. This is a protection for their jobs and also an assurance of quality. If you want non-college staff, tell them who and what their qualifications are. Involve college staff from the early planning stage if possible.

Dr. John Coulter of St. Cloud State University in Minnesota has developed the following criteria for judging workshop content:

1. Is it simple and practical?
2. Will teachers be directly involved in activities themselves, instead of just observing?
3. Is the session relaxed, enjoyable, and non-threatening?
4. Is the equipment easy to make and easy to use?
5. Can the activities be easily altered and taken back to the teacher's class?
6. Is the course providing substantial, worthwhile investigations instead of miscellaneous environmental knowledge and a "mish-mash" of activities?
7. Is there a time regularly set aside for input from the teacher's point of view?
8. Are class members given time to interact informally, exchange ideas, and strengthen each other's confidence?

Do not stay inside to teach about the outside. Be as innovative in conducting your workshop as you are in teaching your classes. If the material is to be used outdoors, do it there. Adjust to weather and environment and demonstrate that the activities that you are promoting do work.

When you are presenting a group of activities, choose the ones that you feel are most important, because studies have demonstrated that 25% of the participants will only use those activities with which they were familiarized in a workshop. Use many activities part way to a conclusion rather than developing all the activities to the maximum. Keep the pace rapid.

Dr. Coulter has written, "There is a direct correlation between the number of actual experiences tried by teachers in any environmental education course and the number of experiences later implemented for students with the teacher's own class."

At the end of a workshop, a printed proceedings is important if the topic was factual. Notes are often lost, blurred or incomplete, and the translation of workshop dialogue into classroom presentations can become distorted if adequate source material is not available. For many people, the option to buy tape recordings is important. Tapes can be listened to while the teacher is driving a car, cooking, or just relaxing, and they require less effort then reading.

Involvement is a key to success in workshops as well as in field trips.

If you are doing an activity workshop, do not just talk about the things you can do—do them! Be excited about what you are doing. Beware of giving away the end result. Set up the activities and let them happen. Keep some mystery and magic in your program. Make the workshop fun.

WORKSHOP CHECK LIST

Tasks Prior to the Workshop

____ Decide to conduct an environmental study area workshop
____ Initiate contact with school system or resource area/agency
____ Decide if college credits are needed. Contact professor.
____ Form steering committee
____ Develop workshop design
     ____ Agree on goals
     ____ Determine objectives in light of goals
     ____ Brainstorm activities to achieve objectives
     ____ Identify limiting factors
     ____ Select activities

_____ Sequence activities
_____ Bad weather alternatives
_____ Identify necessary support systems for activities
_____ Outline general schedule
_____ Make college credit arrangements
_____ Determine cost
_____ Select participants
_____ Determine best means to reach target audience
_____ Select workshop site
_____ Arrange for housing (if necessary), meals, transportation
_____ Contact resource persons
_____ Gather materials
_____ Develop first aid procedures
_____ Determine program troubleshooter who will make quick decisions during the workshop session
_____ Handle publicity
_____ Develop specific schedule
_____ Develop information sheets
_____ Mail advance materials to participants

Tasks During the Workshop

_____ Register participants
_____ Assign rooms (if necessary)
_____ Check meeting places
_____ Provide on-the-spot support
_____ Provide refreshments
_____ Conduct start-up activities
_____ Record the sessions
_____ Evaluate activities
_____ Handle difficult situations

Tasks Following the Workshop

_____ Send in grades (if necessary)
_____ Send thank you notes to those providing assistance
_____ Encourage continued use of the workshop site
_____ Prepare summary report of workshop
_____ Conduct follow-up evaluation

An evaluation process might begin immediately after each workshop session by asking two questions of the participants.

1. Was the workshop run efficiently and effectively?
2. Did the workshop meet your personal needs and expectations?

Have the participants give each question a score of 1–10. If the results are then plotted on a two axis graph, the resulting web will show you how close you came to your 10–10 objective and will show you where a follow-up questionnaire might focus to improve future presentations.

Nine

Spirals

Conservation is a state of harmony between man and land.

ALDO LEOPOLD

The approaches a person brings to teaching must reflect not only personal abilities and classroom goals, but the resources that nature displays. The environment is a dynamic entity and it moves steadily on a path of change. No moment is recoverable, no point in the future will ever duplicate a point in the past. Even the earth's position in the universe is unique only to that moment.

You have noticed that everything an Indian does is in a·circle, and that is because the Power of the World always works in circles, and everything tries to be round. Everything the Power of the World does is done in a circle. The sky is round, and I have heard that the earth is round like a ball, and so are all the stars. The sun comes forth and goes down again in a circle. The moon does the same, and both are round. Even the seasons form a great circle in their changing, and always come back again to where they were.

BLACK ELK, Oglala Sioux

In reading Black Elk's words, we can only begin to understand what he calls "circles" in the natural world. We use the word "cycles" in our everyday vocabulary. We talk of food webs, carbon, nitrogen, life and death, water, calcium, and a hundred other natural cycles, and the rotting log innocently demonstrates what our words stumble to portray.

The Foundation for the Study of Cycles, located in Pennsylvania, has catalogued more than 500 different phenomena in thirty-six different areas of knowledge that fluctuate in rhythmic cycles.

Each event in history is a culmination of the past with the conditions in the present. Craig Blacklock, wildlife photographer, once said, "At a given point in time the cycles appear circular, when extended over time they become spirals." Circles repeat, spirals change.

History is resplendent with examples of spirals. Our great dust bowls of 1934 were a good example. The Southern Great Plains had always been a land of cycles—heat and cold—and with the advent of man, prosperity and poverty.

The plants and animals had learned to use the one year out of ten that rainfall was abundant and the six years out of ten that the land was arid. Life adjusted. Animals that could not adjust moved on, and plants that came when there was abundance, withered and died.

The cycles repeated, but history changed the players. The farmers who came in the 1880s and suffered the drought in 1893 were not as well equipped as the farmers of 1900 who were ruined by the drought of 1911. The increased technology of World War I made the farmers of the 1920s forget the earlier problems until they were decimated by the Dust Bowl of 1933–34.

Natural spirals come in smaller patterns too. There is a spiral

The spirals of the vine tendril are a part of the flow of nature's power.

pattern to the scales in a pine cone; in the path of a brown creeper on a tree trunk; in the coiled tendrils of a vine; and in the shell of a snail.

Humans also see spirals in our individual lives as we reach out, experience, and grow. We have the capacity to expand our knowledge in spirals. We can understand the concepts of change and the rhythms and relationships of the world, and teaching can be augmented by a knowledge of the stepping stones of our earthly spiral: the seasons.

The word "season" is passed to us from the Old French "saison" and the Latin "sation," both of which meant "the action of sowing." Sowing seeds is a necessity for human life and the fluctuation of our seasons determined when the sowing should be done.

In fact, our seasons are astronomical measurements that correspond with the relation of the sun's rays to the earth. We orbit our solar power cell like a great model plane, tilted slightly on our axis. During our annual rounds our position in relation to the sun's rays is altered. Twice a year the sun beats on a direct plane with the equator and we have spring and autumn equinoxes. This position is maintained for only a short time as the relative position of the earth and sun continues to adjust until it reaches the extremes of the Topic of Cancer and Tropic of Capricorn. At these points we have winter and summer solstices. Like all calendars, our seasons are an astronomical measurement.

Of most practical application is the fact that the strength of the sun's rays (their warming potential) is diminished by the angle of the rays in relation to any part of the earth's surface.

In measuring the earth's movement, segments of time had to be devised and the major units were the months. The moon was the major celestial unit for many cultures and months corresponded to the moon's twenty-nine day orbit. The Ojibwas named the full moons, which were the beginning of each new calendar segment, as:

1. The Deep Snow Moon—Ishpagonaga Giziz
2. The Crust of Snow Moon—Onabini Giziz
3. The Snowshoe Breaking Moon—Bekobwedagiming Giziz
4. The Maple Sugar Moon—Iskigamizige Giziz
5. The Budding Plants Moon—Zagibaga Giziz
6. Strawberry Moon—Odelimini Giziz
7. Midsummer Moon—Abitanibi Giziz
8. Harvest Moon—Minike Giziz
9. The Wild Rice Harvest Moon—Manominike Giziz
10. The Falling Leaves Moon—Banakwe Giziz

The sun and the zodiac formed our twelve month calendar. As the earth's rotation placed the sun in alignment with different zodiac characters on the equatorial plane, the months changed. The equatorial plane is an imaginary flat disc extending out from our equator, and the zodiac constellations are neatly aligned with this.

The only good reason to have any measure of time is to meet a need. The most important needs were to provide adequate shelter and food, and the seasons are still our best timetable for that.

Seasons are unique. Seasons are synonomous with change. They are metaphors of emotion and they are mental images. They are precise units of time, yet they transcend those units except to the astronomer and the calendar maker.

Spring, autumn, summer, and winter arrive and depart, indifferent to the calendar, like ancient gods who occasionally grow restless or slumber too long. In some years they even appear to do battle as the transition takes place. Sometimes, to our surprise, a season may appear in the midst of someone else's term like a special guest.

When we speak of seasons, we talk of aging and rebirth, the natural recycling of our world. We find ourselves in the spring of our youth or the autumn of our years, with a fullness in summer and a quiet, non–threatening death in winter.

The northern states are the theatres of seasons, the variety act of geography. Seasons are respected more in the north because they put on a grander act. They add spice to living like seasoning to food. Seasons and seasoning are change—relatively predictable change— but still exciting.

The southern states are seasonal too and northerners tend to forget that winter is not just the accumulation of snow, and spring is not just the melting of that snow. The changes are more subtle, but they are still there. The movement of birds from one area merely means the accumulation of more birds in another area.

Winter, the English form of Old High German "wintar," is defined as the season between autumn and spring, the cold half of the year. It is the dormant season of hibernation and denning. It is the period when many birds and people travel south from the northern climes. It is the time of sub-zero temperatures, the glint of moonbeams on fresh snow, and thousands of tracks telling stories of the wild adventures of hearty northland animals.

A winter study should begin with an understanding of what

The sun moves through the seasons and the universe in a rotating spiral.
COURTESY CRAIG R. BORCK.

winter is in different parts of the world. Exchange letters with students in other states to find out what their winter is like. Newspaper weather services often have world temperature charts which could be plotted on a map to show relative climates.

In the north, snow is the key ingredient to winter. Snowflakes can be captured on black felt that has been cooled to air temperature and the flakes can be observed with magnifying glasses.

W.A. Bentley, a Vermonter who lived from 1865 to 1931, was the "investigator of snowflakes." While a boy he became fascinated with snowflakes and the fact that he could not see any two alike. During his lifetime he took over 5,000 photographs of snowflakes, beginning with an 1880 vintage camera and microscope. He first set up his apparatus in a cold woodshed during a snowstorm and, lacking today's modern equipment, he had to use that setting as his laboratory.

To take his pictures, he would head to his cold room whenever a snowstorm hit the area. He would take a small, black velvet-covered wooden tray with a wire handle and hold it out the open doorway until a few flakes had fallen on it. He would then choose his photographic favorite, and by placing a slender wooden pick in the center of the flake, move it to a microscope slide. Though his hands were massive, his touch was delicate.

Bentley knew what others thought, as well as how he felt. Near the end of his life he remarked, "Some folks call me a fool and probably crazy. They want to know what good it does to get all these pictures of snow. I don't argue with them. I am satisfied. I have got letters from men with lots of letters after their names who know a hundred times more than I do, or than anyone around here, I guess. And those men tell me I'm doing what they call a 'great work.' I don't know about that, but I do know what I like. And I think I see as much around here to enjoy, right here on my own farm, as those who call me a fool. Most of them have never seen a darned thing."

Bentley did see other things—the insects, the mammals, the ferns, and the birds—but he lived for snowstorms and his beloved snowflakes.

Winter is a time of many puzzles. The plants shut down all their systems for six months in the north and they put up with a temperature range of 150 degrees or more. A botanist studying trees in the Rocky Mountains found that pure water inside some hardwoods cooled to −40 degrees F without freezing, because of the sugars in the sap.

In trees like aspen, birch, fir, pine and cedar, the cells can freeze solid without damage because water content drops in the fall and the remaining water is drawn out into the spaces between the cells where it freezes in a huge crystalline mass which does not injure the dessicated cells. Sometimes these ice masses form stress lines and crack. If the pressure is sufficient, we hear popping sounds in the woods when this crack forms, and it is possible to find trees that have split their sides as a result.

Some birds move south, others brave the cold. To stay means very few insects in the diet. Many birds change diet back and forth from insect to seeds with the seasons. To survive at these cold temperatures, the birds depend on trapped air spaces between their feathers to insulate them and they must eat enough food to provide caloric heat. A little redpoll needs to eat 42% of its body weight each day.

Many mammals face this problem too, for only the bats can

Winter is a time of quiet and subtle beauty.

migrate south. The shrew eats its own weight each day to survive. The deer change from a diet of herbaceous plants to that of woody browse. Muskrats swim under the ice, voles live under the snow, and the snowshoe hare uses its big feet to move on the surface of the snow.

The most unique adaptation in mammals is hibernation. Heartbeat is lowered, body temperatures are lower, and some hidden internal clock will motivate the animal when spring arrives. These animals have a special temperature regulating system in their brains and they have the ability to put on large quantities of fat weight in the fall.

Other animals have less obvious winter protection than fur and fat, and these hibernate as well. Snakes form living balls of intertwined bodies beneath the frostline. Small beetles, thrips, spiderlings, bugs, and ants find seclusion in mullein leaves, while mosquito and midge larva are frozen in the ice of a pitcher plant leaf. Mourning cloaks and other insects hide beneath loose bark. Rotting logs hold insects, salamanders, and wood frogs, while other frogs, salamanders, and insects burrow in the mud of ponds and streams.

In this season of odd adaptations, it is even common for snowfleas to appear on warm days and litter the snow like a spilled jar of pepper, or for a stonefly to emerge from a stream and mate.

This is a season of puzzles. A sixth grade class in Pine City, Minnesota, asked these questions regarding winter. How many can you answer?

1. How is snow formed?
2. Why are snowflakes perfectly formed?
3. How come snow is small?
4. Why does it snow?
5. How does snow turn white?
6. Why is snow cold?
7. Why does it snow in some places and not in others?
8. Why doesn't it snow when it is −30 degrees F?
9. How come snow doesn't melt when it hits the ground?
10. How come sometimes it snows a little and sometimes a lot?
11. How come roads in the country melt faster than roads in the city?
12. Why doesn't it snow in gobs?
13. How can snow insulate?
14. Is hail like snow?
15. What would happen if it didn't snow in Minnesota?
16. Why does snow turn to ice?
17. Why does snow melt in your hand, but not in your mitt?
18. Why does ice stay on top of water instead of sinking?
19. How does snow begin?
20. How and why do snowshoes stay on top of snow?
21. How are snowshoes made?
22. Can artificial snow be used without harming the land?
23. How do your make artificial snow? ice?
24. How long can a person live below zero?
25. If stalled in a snowstorm, how long could you live?
26. How long could you live in a snowcave without food or water?
27. Is the earth closer or farther away from the sun in winter?
28. Why does winter come at the same time each year?
29. Why does winter come?
30. Why is the air so cold in winter and hot in summer?
31. Why doesn't the hot sun's rays keep the ground from freezing?
32. Why does the temperature suddenly change?
33. Why do lakes "turn over"?
34. Why does frost come before snow?
35. Why is it colder on sunny days and warmer on cloudy days?

36. Why is it so cold in winter?
37. What is the purpose of winter?
38. How did winter get its name?
39. How do animals live in winter? Do they like winter?
40. Why do some birds fly south?
41. Why don't dogs hibernate?
42. Do any birds hibernate?
43. How come animals don't die when they hibernate?
44. How can the birds stand winter?
45. How does a rabbit find food in the winter?
46. Why doesn't the fox hibernate?
47. How and why does a rabbit change color in winter?
48. When the ice forms on a lake, what happens to the fish?
49. How do squirrels know when to gather food?
50. How do beaver survive in ice locked homes?
51. How do animals know when it is time to hibernate?
52. How do ants and worms spend the winter?
53. How do grass and green things live through the winter?
54. Why do plants stop growing in winter?
55. Why don't trees die in the winter?
56. Does tree bark change color in the winter?
57. Do trees breathe during winter?

The sounds of winter are the chickadee calls, the swish of skis, and the sharp sound of a frost cracked tree. The mood of winter is freshness, purity, and beauty. Color winter white.

Spring comes from Old High German "springan" which meant "to jump" and the Greek "sperchesthai," which means "to hasten." Spring means to be resilient, to grow, to come into being, a water source, the season between winter and summer. This is the season of inspiration. We have the classic March struggles between the lions and the lambs, followed by the maple sap flowing and the swelling buds. There is a flood of white woodland flowers, like the snows have come alive, and there is a burst of fresh green everywhere. The world washes itself in rains, frogs serenade life, and young animals can be found everywhere.

The outdoor classroom is alive with ideas now, but the teacher must know the sequence. Fish spawn in the streams and the riffles are alive with scaly backs. Most fishermen will know when this happens in their area.

Spring is a time of youth and energy.

Early spring is the time to look for the skunk cabbage to push its flowers up through the snow. This flower has its own internal furnace and actually melts the snow and soil where it emerges.

The woody plants tend to flower first and most of these flowers have pollen instead of nectar, which the bees gather for the hive. Hawks hunt on barren fields where the weight of the winter's snow has matted down the grasses. The tunnels and nests of the mice and voles look like maps in the field and can be studied and mapped by a class.

The mourning cloak emerges from hibernation and adds a touch of early color to the woods. Seed eating birds follow the hawks north and chipmunks come out of hibernation.

Temporary pools in the fields and woods come alive with insects and plankton. The sun's heat is absorbed by the decaying plant material on the pond's bottom and the water is warm while the air remains cool. Woodcocks sing and do their dance, as do the grouse and prairie chicken. The saps run and the maple sugar bush begins to operate.

Woodland flowers soon replace maple sap buckets, insects emerge, and the air is filled with colorful wings and cheery songs as the birds migrate back to the north. Frogs sing and mate, bees gather nectar, nests are built, turtles and snakes come out, and the leaves appear on the trees.

Each event in its turn is a study in itself; each day has a freshness. Spring fever is a contagious and the teacher should try to capitalize on this.

There is a healthy odor to the fertile soil and the trees are decorated with feathery bursts of color. This season is filled with song and gaity. Color spring green.

Summer is another Old High German word, "sumer." In Sanskrit it was "sama," meaning year or season. There is a maturity to the world now. Most foliage is blooming or past bloomed. Photosynthesis has taken place and new buds are forming for next year. Butterflies abound in the fields, dancing a ballet to the sophisticated concerts of grasshoppers, cicadas, and crickets.

In the richness of this season there is time to devote a summer school class to a complete study or to an expedition. This is a season for accomplishment.

Water is a source of pleasure and use, but also a chance for study. Hypsometers, calculation of dewpoint, and cloud studies introduce

Summer is richness and green.

moisture in the air, and solar stills show moisture in the ground, but the real source of study is in the pond or in the lake. Map the basin, complete simple chemical tests, use minnow traps, seines, plankton tows, and bottom dredges to sample organisms. Fishing or snorkeling activities could also be used.

Identify other animal life around the water, including birds, mammals, reptiles, amphibians, insects, snails, and clams. Map the groupings of plants on shore and in the water. Compare your results with another lake or pond, marsh, river, ocean or bog.

Go canoeing. Visit water treatment plants. Go swimming. Have a fun time while learning.

This is the season that fills the center of the year with an edible bounty and a lust for living. Color summer gold with goldenrod, sunflowers, trefoil, St. Johnswort, and black-eyed susans on a field of green.

Autumn, from the Latin "autumn," is the season between summer and winter, a period of maturity or incipient decline. Brook trout and brown trout spawn in the fall. As the day length duplicates its spring counterpart, frogs and birds often do half-hearted versions of their spring song and dance routines, a phenomenon called "false spring."

Migration is southerly, apples ripen, bucks rub the velvet from their antlers, puffballs send smoke signals all over the woods. Leaves change colors and fall to the ground. Squirrels gather acorns, rock ferns curl up, and common animals disappear, one by one.

On warm days, snakes move into the pavement for one last warming, witch hazel is the last plant to flower, the taste of cranberries and persimmons benefit from a freeze. Snowshoe hares and weasels change from brown to white, puddles look like broken window panes, and flocks of crows gather in leafless treetops and brown fields with broken pumpkin shells.

There is a mellowness in the frosty air, a melancholy in the rustling leaves. We know autumn for its briskness, the ice on the puddles, and the waterfowl in the air. The sounds of the season are muted honks heard above the dry rattle of windblown burr oak leaves. Color autumn with bright orange sugar maples, red oaks and sumacs, and yellow birch.

These four seasons are the products of astronomy and calendars, civilizations, and individuals. We know them and accept them, yet there are two more seasons that correspond with the midway point in the sun's equinox/solstice travels. Let us call these times the solstinoxes.

I am susceptible to the seasons like everyone else, but my seasonal clock has certain peaks and I shift gears six times a year. Winter begins with the snow that stays. Winter: snow. They are synonymous to this naturalist and I think winter right up to the next season: melt. Melt is the rain, warm, freeze, snow period of indecision. Do I need more snow or am I anxious for the flowers? This is a time of cold, wet feet, slogging without ski or snowshow in snow that is ninety percent water.

Spring begins when the buds burst. It is a magical time of daydream, love, and flights of fancy. It is the moment the ice goes out, the first notes of the veery, the cheery bloom of the hepatica. It comes suddenly and passes quickly. Everything is green and then it is summer.

Summer begins in May most years, and goes on until September. Then frost checks the green and some plants go into a frenzy of color as a last farewell to summer.

Autumn is the time of color, with color in the trees and in the golden fields of grass. Then clouds build in the west, like a magic wand, and winds send the color from the plants and the leaves from the trees. Bleak, black silhouettes stand against the grey sky, branches clattering in the whistling nor'westers. Waves whip furiously in Great Lake storms, and ice sculptures paint the rocky shores. This is the sixth season: fall.

The spiral makes another bend and we enter the winter, melt, spring, summer, autumn, fall sequence again. Each period is startling and impressive, and each has a volume of studies, lessons and feelings, if we will only stop and watch.

Ten

Bad Weather and Fears

Winds are whispering in the balsams, singing softly in the cedars, crooning through the glistening birches—sleep, little warrior, sleep.

MENOMINEE INDIAN CRADLE SONG

Scientists claim that we are born with only two fears; loud noises and falling. All other fears are developed. This means that humans are cultivating their fears of spiders, insects, large animals like wolves and bears, unusually shaped animals like the octopus, animals of the dark, like bats, and animals of the deep, such as the shark. Fairy tales give form to our fears of the dark and the unknown. Civilizations use the fear of the unknown to discipline and control children. These fears are reinforced by television and movie figures like Dracula, the shark in "Jaws," and other references to "the swamp," "werewolves," "vampire bats," and "the deep, dark, woods."

Perhaps worst of all is the inevitable campfire story and the laughter of "adult" leaders who relish the insecurity of a young child's imagination when they tell of ghosts and monsters in the woods, instead of painting pictures of beauty and peace. How much better would the child sleep at night after hearing, instead, canoe country naturalist Sigurd Olson's story of "The Dream Net"?

A Chippewa woman presented Sigurd with a dream net of fine

thread strung tightly to a four inch hoop of ash, like a spider web with a perfect quarter inch circle in the center. This net was to be hung over the sleeping child where it would trap bad dreams, but let good dreams in. As she explained to Olson, the good dreams came through the net, but the bad dreams were tangled in the mesh, and when the light struck them in the morning, they died.

Since then Olson writes, "I have seen it in interlacing branches overhead, in hovering cliffs and in snow-clad peaks of mountain ranges, even in the stars themselves."

Our outdoor education should instill respect and encourage curiosity. Fears contradict everything we stand for. Teach the students the skills they need to be comfortable in the wilds. Teach them self-reliance so that they have confidence in themselves. Challenge them to be part of nature, and discourage the image of conquering the wilds.

The compass and map are two tools of self-reliance that can be used to learn about the land as well as to build confidence in the individual. Let the students carry a map and compass on field trips and then step off the trails. Let them see that imminent danger does not surround them. Establish an aura of discovery. Take note of the objects to which you react and learn more about them. Watch those things which seem scary or repulsive, take their pictures, draw them, take a closer look at them, and then use references and resource people to learn more about them. See if knowing about something helps to diminish many of the fears. Let the students lead you in and out of the woods with their compass skills.

Plan your trip as safe as you would an expedition. Have the students make an itinerary and file a route plan with the school or nature center office. Make an agreement about what to do if an individual gets lost from the group. Practice getting lost and finding your way.

Have everyone dress properly for the outing; those that do not should not be allowed to go along. (See Appendix for wet weather gear.)

Teach the students what animals do in bad weather by going out in it. Rain may be discomforting only because it is never encountered as a positive experience. Whom amongst us can survive without water? What plants can grow or what animals can survive without moisture? Rain can be fun.

A group of students, caught in the throes of an all-day rain, had no choice but to make the most of the day and learn what rain was all about. They began by analyzing what they had to work with and came up with this list of questions.

1. Is there anything in rain besides water?
2. How big are raindrops?
3. How hard do raindrops hit?
4. What do the animals do when it rains?
5. Are there places that are wetter or drier?
6. How far into the ground does rain go?
7. What do the animals in the lake do?
8. How does rain affect the attitudes of people?
9. Do you get wetter or drier by running in the rain?
10. What is the best place for a shelter from the rain?
11. How do you build a fire in the rain?
12. What do bees do when it rains?
13. Is there life in a puddle?

Thoreau said that rainy days were his favorite days because only those people who cared about nature the most would be out and he could find more solitude in the wet woods.

How do others react to this phenomenon? What do people normally do when it rains? How are their moods affected?

The students appointed a resident psychiatrist to interview people in and out of the class to learn the psychological implications of rain, and the rest of the class went wild trying out rain activities.

Into a folded piece of art paper went powdered tempera paints. When the paper was held flat with one side raised ninety degrees, the droplets of water would hit the painters and send splatters on the upraised side. This was a study of impact and splash.

A box of plaster of paris caught different sized raindrops. Students went bird watching, fishing, took plankton samples, and had a great day in the rain. They reported to each other and shared their knowledge.

There is a delicacy to rain that can be observed as drops fall from leaf to leaf on their way to the ground or hit upon puffballs, sending clouds of spores into the air.

A class can make a musical instrument by placing empty cans of various sizes on a board, allowing the rain droplets to hit on the can bottoms. Each size will give a different tone and the eaves will play different music than the open field. You can even play songs by covering up some cans and letting the rain hit only certain tone producers.

Stand on a beach where you can watch the rain march across the water or the wind make the surface dance. Watch lightning strike in

All weather has its charm and excitement if we accept it and make the most of what is available.

the distance. Listen to the rumbles and learn about another fear maker. The ancients used to believe that lightning was the fire of heavenly dragons and the waves were produced by the heaving of giant sea dragons.

Extend discovery to the dark. Take a hike through a forest or field at night and then retrace the hike in the daylight. Use a rope with knots every ten feet to keep the group well spaced, but still in contact with one another. Safety goggles for protecting eyes are an important safety consideration. Listen, walk quietly, and have a rope signal to instruct everyone to stop and sit quietly.

Night time was a veil that swallowed the light of day for people who lived in ancient times of intellectual darkness. It distorted lines and images and magnified the frailty of humans. The stars and the moon were beacons or the eyes of divinity, and early mankind looked for knowledge in heavenly and earthbound light sources.

Today those fears seem less substantial and our knowledge of the universe should allow us to move with more security and let us search out the discoveries that are part of night.

Our fear of the night comes from the loss of the sense we rely on most: sight. Humans feel helpless when deprived of the visual images that their world has been built on, yet blind people function well in this world. If the fear of night were anything more, the blind should feel it too, but they don't, they only sense the discomfort of the sighted.

Sounds seem eerie because we become more aware of them as the other senses expand to fill the niche that belongs to the eyes in the daylight. Our perception is distorted from disuse and we substitute fear for understanding.

Vision becomes more acute as time passes on a night exploration. Leave flashlights for leaders only and for emergency use only. Rather than giving confidence, fires and flashlight beams isolate people from the woods even more. They constrict the experience to the parameters of the light, emphasizing shadows which become grotesque and caricatured, making the surrounding area seem even darker and more foreboding. In addition, any light source retards the development of night vision.

With understanding, night becomes a change of perspective, not a time of fear. Dawn and dusk will be seen as the shaded parts of a day that stand between the two great contrasts.

Death is symbolized by darkness in our civilization and night is a poetic metaphor in literature that perpetuates our fear of both. This is the fear of the unknown, the same terror that prohibits the inner city youth from walking into the big woods. The outdoor classroom is a tool for exploring other realms of the unknown; perhaps it can even help us understand the role of death.

The owl is a symbolic animal in the folklore of almost every part of the globe. It has been used to symbolize both night and death. As recently as the 1970s it was used to foretell death. In Margaret Craven's *I Heard The Owl Call My Name*, the Eskimos' belief that the owl is a precursor to death was the premise for the title and a part of the tale.

Shakespeare used the owl as a symbol in more than one play.

The first great naturalist of the civilized world, Pliny the Elder, took the beliefs that preceeded him and attempted to make them fact when he wrote:

> When it appears (the owl) fortells nothing, but evil, and if auspices which import the public zeal are being taken at the time, is more to be dreaded than any bird . . . it prognosticates dire misfortunes.

The early Chinese called the owl the bird that snatches the soul. The Aztecs placed the hearts of their sacrifices in an owl-shaped statue. Romans, Greeks, Egyptians, Australians, and even the cave painters of Les Trois Frères in France used symbols of owls in their places of dwelling.

The owl is a symbol of death in legend, but it is both exciting and important in reality.

Each culture was exploring its own fear of death with the conqueror of darkness: the owl. To replace such an ingrained symbolism is a mighty task.

In the study of death we need to explore its relationship with life. The rotting log is alive with moss, seedlings, and animals in larval and adult forms. Many mushrooms and saprophytes, like squawroot, Indian pipe, and pinesap, need dead and decaying tissues for life. The soil is alive with plant and animal life that change the decaying plant matter into the humus which, in turn, supports new plants.

Death is all around us in the natural world and in the outdoor classroom. Nature center shelves are lined with heads and feet, specimens and remnants, yet the word death is seldom spoken. In nature the rotting log nurses the seedlings, the dead animal feeds the living, and death seems to be a requirement for life.

An elementary teacher in Florida uses a cemetery as her outdoor classroom for a study of death. The class is exploring a great taboo, something mysterious and frightening. They write wills, obituaries, and gravestone epitaphs; they visit a mortuary to observe a dead person.

ANNA EDSTROM
AGED 36 YEARS
REGINA AGED 10 YEARS
WERNER AGED 7 YEARS
LILLIE AGED 3 YEARS
MARTHA AGED 1 YEAR
Wife & Children of
ERRIK EDSTROM
Burned to death at
Sandstone Minn. Sept 1, 1894.

Human history is recorded in the cemetery. This family was caught in the Great Hinckley Fire.

As early as 1915 a researcher named Pearson saw the urban cemetery as a bird sanctuary. In 1977, a new study was published on the same subject, based on ten cemeteries in Chicago. In all of the studies, the cemeteries provided refuges for birds from the surrounding urban environment. Perhaps if development goes unabated, the cemeteries will be the parks of future generations.

A good source book for understanding the cycles of nature is *Understanding the Game of the Environment*, Agriculture Information Bulletin No. 426, available from the Superintendent of Documents, Washington, D.C.

Loren Eiseley, in *The Unexpected Universe*, paints a part of the picture in the following revelation:

> Before turning to that realm of shadows, it is well to define what we mean by the web of life. Some time ago I had occasion one summer morning to visit a friend's grave in a country cemetery. The event made a profound impression upon me. By some trick of midnight circumstance a multitude of graves in the untended grass were covered and interwoven together in a shimmering sheet of gossamer, whose threads ran indiscriminately over sunken grave mounds and headstones.

It was as if the dead were still linked as in life, as if that frail network, touched by the morning sun, had momentarily succeeded in bringing the inhabitants of the grave into some kind of persisting relationship with the living. The intricate web in which past life is intertwined with all that lives and in which the living constitute a subtle, though not totally inescapable, barrier to any newly emergent creature that might attempt to break out of the enveloping strands of the existing world.

The aura of mystery that surrounds death cannot be eliminated, but the acceptance of death as a natural part of life can be taught.

Children should be exposed to death—it is not something to ignore.

In comparison with the fears of death, darkness, and the unknown, other fears seem minor, but no fear is inconsequential to the person who suffers from it. Insects are always present. Their pestiness is something which must be accepted partially as a condition of being outside, but for some those fears go beyond irritation.

What do people fear in insects? They do not like the feeling of things crawling on their skin. They have been warned as a child, "Don't let the bed bugs bite!" Most insects are ugly in human terms, with too many parts in weird arrangements. People have heard stories about killer bees and malaria mosquitoes. Maybe the most important factor is that we don't like to be outnumbered.

It might be beneficial to take your class to visit a beekeeper, to learn what pollinates, as well as what eats, the garden crops. We need to understand why some people eat insects,. We need to understand that some insects specialize in eating the kinds that we do not like.

We also need to understand how prolific insects are. Those we consider pests are able to adapt to poisons and repellents, while the insects that eat the mosquito and the fly are predators that reproduce less and are more sensitive to chemical warfare.

Repellents are applied to the skin to ward off insects, but they are poisons that pollute the land, air, and water, and can irritate the human as well as the insect. A class should have a rule against aerosol repellents, because the repellent is easily carried by the breeze and will land on non-selective targets. It should also prohibit the use of repellents when doing aquatic studies, for the poison will come off in the water and kill the organisms that are being studied.

Use insect netting, lightweight clothing that eliminates exposed skin surface, and the wind and sun, as deterrents. If repellents are needed, use them on clothing rather than skin. Learn about the source of the fears, rather than reacting in a way that is self-destructive.

The fear of spiders is similar to the fear of insects. The usual response to the question "Why are you afraid of spiders?" is, "They're creepy and ugly!" Spiders are also very poorly understood. Why do they spin webs? Do they poison people?

Spiders are insect eaters, so they are on our side when it comes to flies and mosquitoes, yet people fear them as much as any animals that we know. These fierce-looking predators are masters of design. The webs can be studied with cameras and sketch pads. The spider can be raised in an aquarium and students can study its behavior. Model webs can be made using colored yarn, and used to decorate the entire class ceiling. The *Golden Guide's Spider Book* is a good guide for making a web.

The web is part of the source of fear. A tacky web across the face in a dark woods is an unexpected, strange feeling. Horror films have exploited the ten foot web in the dark jungle as a source of human danger, adding to our fears.

Spiders also seem to sneak up on us. They make no noticeable sounds and they move softly, but they will not attack humans. In fact, only the brown recluse and the black widow spiders can be considered poisonous, and the big hairy tarantula is not only nonpoisonous, but is a secretive hermit that is extremely difficult to find.

In some Indian mythology the spider is represented in the sky by the constellation we know as the Corona Borealis, its threads forming the Milky Way. In nature, its threads are an intricate part of a much larger web.

Ticks are neither spiders nor insects, and they are difficult for even the most avid nature fan to admire, but it is also difficult to justify being afraid of them. They are creepy, they are not pretty, they suck blood, and they sometimes carry disease, but they can be grasped firmly, pulled off, and discarded.

Why do we fear snakes? The snake is silent, it creeps, and it is the symbol of evil in the Garden of Eden. Some snakes are poisonous, some appear to be slimy, some are gigantic, and all have been exploited by the media. In legends, the serpent monsters were feared because of their rapid movements, the swiftness of their attack, and their venom. They hid in secret places and were able to shed their old skins and put on new ones, thereby possessing eternal youth. They must have been sustained by magic, for they were seldom seen to eat.

The most effective way to dispel the myths might be to handle a snake. Show students that they are not slimy by having a snake crawl through a sandy area and then have the student place his/her hand in the same sand. The body of the snake will be clean, but sand will cling to the hand.

Snakes are really non-aggressive, and most are non-poisonous. They cannot steal milk from cows, grab their own tails and roll down hills like a hoop, or hypnotize observers. In fact, they are so nonviolent that the territorial fight of rattlesnakes is a form of arm wrestling in which the two opponents intertwine the upper halves of their bodies; the snake who gets his head pinned gives up the battle and all rights to the territory.

The human fear of large animals is usually a result of more mythology or tall tales. People attribute the human qualities of reasoning, revenge, and meanness to larger animals and fear them for those reasons.

Most fears are due to a lack of knowledge and a lack of understanding. Help the students believe they are a part of nature. Help

*Bad Weather
and Fears*

them be confident of their own ability to survive in the woods and help make their entire learning experience a positive one. Be prepared as a teacher to handle the unexpected, accept the conditions that disappoint, and share a love of the outdoors. Turn a fear into a source of learning and maybe the fear will go away.

Eleven

Tread Lightly

When I return from any wilderness expedition, it is always a shock to encounter the sounds of civilization. It is almost as though I had stepped into a different world, so swift and strident does it seem. When it is more than I can bear, I stroll into the woods to recapture what I had left behind.

SIGURD OLSON

We provide our greatest lesson in land ethics by the way we treat the area we are studying. Nothing is more influential than the impact of our own actions. If we justify destruction and modification for the purpose of study, we have a poor argument to halt destruction for other reasons.

A nature center can be looked at in two ways. It can be a point of convergence or a point of divergence. In the first instance it is the key location in which all studies are done, and in the second, it is a meeting point, the spot of gathering, and from there the group will go to appropriate study places.

For a drop-in and day use center, convergence must be expected and design should reflect this. For a resident center or camp, either alternative is possible.

A study site must also reflect the visitation policy. If an area is open to drop-in visitation only, it may develop a casual trail system which allows for people dispersal through many interconnected loops and alternatives. In this way, individuals can feel a sense of discovery and exploration by putting together their own course. It encourages the person to return since the multiple trail combinations offers variety, and leaves a spark of curiosity ("I wonder what's on that trail") in the hiker.

If the area is serving classes, the trails may be a means of dispersing different groups, minimizing the impact of many feet within a frequently used area, and allowing the teacher to feel secure about where the group is and how to get back out. In this instance, trails should not only be dispersed to prevent sound and visual overlap of groups, but they should also reflect the variety of the site and should enable the teacher to choose specific studies for each trail option.

In a combination of drop-in and school class operations, it is ideal to separate school use from public trails to avoid interruption of class studies and to avoid the impact of meeting a group while seeking solitude.

Northwoods Audubon Center in Minnesota is an example of a divergence center. The group size is limited to twenty or less, programs are residential, and three out of five days are spent in study locations on public land near the Center. Programs on the property are not limited to trails, and group use can be monitored and dispersed, allowing impact to be absorbed by the woods.

This is primarily "people" management, a system that is useful only in a few situations, whereas most plans must emphasize resource management.

A trail can be used for movement from point to point, or to disperse groups and individuals. It can also be used for exploration, in which case each stop is equally important: no end point or climax need be designed into the system.

Point-to-point trails are typical of parks, forests, and areas where people walk to a vista, waterfall, or campsite. The trail should be designed to avoid danger and erosion, and is generally a direct line with just a few curves to break up the tunnel effect of a straight swath.

Dispersal systems must consider the volume of users and the carrying capacity of the land. Studies should be done before placing trails in order to determine visual corridors within the ecosystem. Visual corridors equal the distance on each side of the trail that can be seen by a human hiker. In areas of dense vegetation there is a screening effect that limits vision, but in open woodlands, prairies, or along shorelines, the distance can be very great.

If two trails should be placed in the same woods, visual corridors should not overlap, and if you want natural animal movement within the area you must leave a zone between the visual corridors that allows the animal to move freely. They often have better eyesight than humans.

Because some people come to a nature center to experience solitude, shorelines and prairie areas must use further visual planning. Natural contours provide the best planning aids and trails should be strategically placed to keep hills or even slight land rise between them to limit contact between people.

Valleys confine vision and screen parallel groups if one trail is in the valley and a second trail is placed beyond the plane of vision. On waterways it is best to have trails along only one shore, and if a loop is desired, have the trail move away from the lake to return to the starting point.

Visual corridors change with the seasons. Leaves are a major factor in visual screening and when they are gone good summer trails become crowded winter trails. For this reason, winter is often the best season for actual trail layouts.

The placement and use of trails is a complicated procedure if you want the best possible system. When trails are in place, they last a long time. One year of disuse does not eliminate them, and poorly placed trails will plague an area for years. If possible, use a location without trails for four seasons and see where the people walk. On a master map keep track where the teachers and naturalists like to be and plan that into your final system.

Planning can also be an adventure in learning and the involvement of teachers, naturalists, students, and volunteers, can mean discovery and a sense of accomplishment. In addition, those who have a psychological investment in the area will support the program in times of need.

Planning is often improved by teamwork. The job has many facets, and people with different expertise can be called on to survey birds, butterflies, rocks, and plants. These people are often involved in clubs; the local university and library can help you find out how to contact them.

The planning team should encompass many backgrounds and interests, and should visit other outdoor sites before beginning their work. Talk to people who have sites and learn from them. Ask them what works and what does not.

If a school wants its own study site, the planning committee should examine the schoolyard for places that can be converted into natural areas. This study must include a map of existing structures, vegetation, traffic patterns of the school grounds, and the wind and shade affect of the structures.

Ponds can be dug, plantings can be done, and blinds can be built, as well as feeders and animal homes. The shop students and the community can be involved in altering the human impact of the area.

If an environmental site is selected that is adjacent to the school building, transportation time and scheduling are less burdensome. If this is not feasible, the nature centers, parks, and preserves make outstanding outdoor classrooms.

The Nature Conservancy, a national organization concerned with the preservation of many natural and scientific sites, uses the following preserve data list to keep track of their sites. It might serve as a good checklist for environmental study sites as well.

To begin your field planning, enlarge the topographic map for your location and superimpose a grid over it. The grid system is helpful in establishing a location for your notes.

The following field note list is an example of the type of information you might want to gather. The indicators are things which need to be avoided when putting in the trail. The special considerations are conditions which might provide comfort in intense heat or cold or times of insect discomfort. Mark a letter next to each item you find and put that letter on the grid map to mark the exact location. This will give you both a map and a key.

FIELD NOTES FOR PRELIMINARY SITE ASSESSMENT

Physical characteristics of site to be considered.

Predominant timber types:
Dominant understory plants:
Types of animals expected:
Water areas:
   swamp   pond
   bog   lake
   marsh   stream

Percent:
   aquatic   open
   terrestrial   wooded

Special characteristics:
   rock outcrop   nests
   rare plant   other (describe)

Human impact:
   crops   gravel pit
   plantation   other
   road

Indicators:
   drainage route   poison ivy
   mud   nettles

mosquito area   thorny plants
steep slopes   other (describe)
nesting areas
Safety considerations:
   overhanging limbs   rocks
   water current   other
Special considerations:
   shady area
   sunny area
   windy area
Natural trails:
   old roads
   animal made
   openings for group gatherings

Before concluding your background studies, do an aesthetic inventory. Mark, on a map, the special places that each individual on the study team has found. List what made it special. Was it a seasonal phenomenon or would that same feeling always be there? Is it a feeling for individuals only or could it be experienced by a group as well? Where are the best sunrise and sunset views? Where do birds concentrate on migrations?

Meld the background information together and draw trails on paper to see how they look. Do not try to get everyone to every place. Trails concentrate use; they lose all their vegetation due to compaction; they widen in the wet periods because compaction creates a depression which concentrates water; and they are an umbilical cord to a parking lot, building, or other vestiges of civilization. No trails means monitoring or trampling. Be concerned with group dynamics and gathering spots, as well as the fragility of individual areas.

Put turns in your trail to cut hikers off from the visual impact of other groups on the same trail, but avoid sharp corners that encourage cutoffs and widen the impact. Many times the path of least resistance is the most appropriate one to take. Follow the natural contours, avoid steep inclines, keep the trail narrow and intimate, and try to use natural materials, such as rocks placed as stepping stones to cross wet areas.

Steep grades should have switchbacks rather than straight trails to prevent soil erosion and hiker fatigue. The corners and outside edges of these switchbacks might be reinforced with logs laid parallel to the route and held in place by rocks or wooden wedges. In addition to the outside support, log poles can be set in the trail at right angles to stop the flow of soil from water runoff. The poles should be partially buried and staked in the ground in this system.

Trail surfaces can be mowed and left alone, but limestone chips and wood chips are two methods of providing some drainage. On a steep grade, gutters can be cut to allow water to run off to the side.

Across swamps and wet areas, boardwalks can be intimate trail designs. In shallow areas, posts can be driven into the soil to serve as pilings. Pole stringers can then extend from piling to piling, and a walking surface of wood planks can be placed across the stringers. This is a simple dock design and can be extended across a marsh or a swamp.

Floating boardwalks are good for fluctuating water levels and the bouyancy adds an extra feeling for the water area. Wood Lake Nature Center in Richfield, Minnesota, has had a long floating boardwalk for many years and their major problem was the muskrats' desire to use the styrofoam for their lodges. The center is now looking into alternate floatation.

The development of winter trails needs further consideration. A study of ski touring in the Minneapolis/St. Paul area by Charles Smith, park planner, showed that factors which increase the skiers' satisfaction ranked:

1. Good snow conditions
2. Interesting natural area
3. Good trail layout and design
4. Lack of crowds
5. Support facilities

The skiers' satisfaction decreased by the following ranked factors:

1. Poor trail maintenance
2. Poor snow
3. Poor layout and design
4. Lack of support facilities
5. Restrictive rules

The overwhelming reason for choosing an area to ski was convenience. Way below convenience, the following factors influenced trail choice.

1. Other people's influence
2. Trail layout and design
3. Curiosity about new areas
4. Familiarity

A study by Marvin Kottke, professor at the University of Connecticut, shows that cross country skiing in the northeast will increase through the 1980s, regardless of energy problems. This is a home based recreation available throughout the snow belt.

Newby and Lilley, in a University of Maine study, give us the following profile of a cross country skier:

1. Median age: 30–34
2. Skis 20 percent more often on weekends than weekdays (27 days total per year)
3. Goes three miles per hour
4. Sixty percent prefer groomed trails
5. Twenty-eight percent prefer marked trails only
6. Twelve percent prefer neither marked nor groomed
7. Fifty-seven percent are males, 43% are females
8. Thirty-eight percent are single, 56% are married, 6% are divorced
9. Average age of children—12 years old
10. Seventy-one percent were introduced to cross country skiing by family or friends

The cross country skier considers the sport to be close to nature, as well as a pleasant activity. The skier considers snowshoeing, winter camping, and ice fishing as compatible sports, but hunting and snowmobiling should never be mixed with cross country, the great majority believe. This is important to consider in all trail planning.

Since most skiers value the quietness of their sport, trails should not overlap in sound or sight, and there should be adequate trails to disperse skiers. Most studies recommend the distance of 5 kilometers to be the average day ski.

Since flowers are absent and birds are not as prevalent as in the spring through fall landscape, the planner must look to more subtle aesthetic changes in laying out a winter trail. The terrain should vary and the trail should alternate settings (forest types and openings) to provide contrasts.

Slopes can be fun, as well as hazardous, so areas are needed to "run out" or stop. Straight lines are tunnels and lack the pleasant quality of curving trails, but too many turns eliminate glide and skiing pleasure.

Clearing trails for winter use requires an estimation of normal snowfall. Since compacted snow will raise the skier or snowshoer from normal ground level, some consideration must be made for overhead clearance.

Following are some other considerations unique to the winter trail:

1. Wind screening: Coniferous trees block more wind than deciduous. The effect of a natural wind barrier is similar to the effect of a snowfence. Wind will eddy behind the barrier and deposit loose snow.
2. Dark surfaces and artifical surfaces absorb more heat and increase melting.
3. Pines south of a trail negate some sun melting, and trees on the north side may increase melt by the absorption of heat on dark surfaces.
4. Trails that lead directly into the prevailing wind increase discomfort and the possibility of frostbite.

When these ideas have been considered and your plan is on paper, discuss it one more time. Where does the trail begin and end? Are these the best places? How will it be affected by seasons? Can people use the trail without having signs posted all over the woods? Who is responsible for monitoring its use? Who is responsible for upkeep if trees are blown down? Will you have maps to hand out or just one large display map? How will people know the trail rules? Do you want any part of the trail to be self-guiding?

A self-guided trail is a special challenge to a naturalist. Do people learn more from a trail that relies on identification or from a theme? Can you build a trail that emphasizes a concept? Can you make a brochure that is like a story and is so fascinating that people will want to get to each point to see how it comes out?

Be creative in the self-guided trail. Let the reader make up the end of the story and turn it in. A blank area at the end of the brochure is all that is needed. You can collect the used brochures this way and have fascinating reading at the same time.

Put together a collection of thoughts and quotations in a brochure and choose appropriate locations along the trail for people to read these passages. The material in the brochure will be enjoyable whether the people are on the trail or are at home.

The self-guided trail interpretation can be done with signs or notations in a trail guide. Each is appropriate depending on the purpose, and they can be used together in the same trail to add to understanding.

Signs eliminate printing costs, can be easily changed, and can alleviate the litter and distribution problems that are created by handing out brochures. On the other hand, they are easily vandalized, can be overlooked, and need maintenance. Plants that are identified with signs need to be checked for their condition and the density of competing vegetation on a regular basis to prevent confusion and misinformation.

Interpretive stations along a trail must be identified in a way that is easy to locate, but is also unobtrusive, and they must indicate where you should be in the brochure's text. This means signs or markers, which increase cost. Since markers are usually plain, they are less likely to be subject to vandalism, and the brochure may have souvenir and reading value.

A trail that is designed to use landmarks makes the brochure a map as well as a text, eliminates vandalism, and offers challenge and adventure, but it also depends on the visitor's ability to pay attention and follow directions.

A combination trail enables the hiker to get both a story and details. The brochure should tell the story, while signs fill in facts and identification.

If the trail is to be used by handicapped people, there are other

A trail should blend with its surroundings and make the hikers feel as though they are a part of the environment, not on a corridor through it.

things to consider. Not every place can be or should be made available to all handicapped people. If the special requirements of the physically handicapped mean that the trail will detract from the natural conditions, the trail might not be justified. The handicapped person does not want to eliminate experiences for the non-handicapped in the wilderness, nor do they want to experience an area that is so changed to accommodate them that they cannot experience nature.

There is no simple set of rules that encompasses all trails and handicapped problems, but one rule must be adhered to in all situations: never call attention to a person's handicap. One study of handicapped trails related that a trail should not emphasize a single disability, such as blindness or old age. Facilities developed for a certain handicapped group and labeled as such often provoke feelings of inferiority and segregation. Whenever possible, make trails that fit all people.

Jonathan Schwartz, of the State University of New York, in a study entitled "Report on Investigation of Natural Trails for the Visually Impaired", writes,

> If there is a guide rope along a trail, both the sighted and the visually impaired can use them together. But in this case integration is achieved at the cost of some of the "naturalness" of the experience for the sighted. One normally does not find three fourth inch bright yellow rope strung through the woods. The rope is not only unnatural, it can be an actual barrier between people and nature. Set up at waist height, a rope or railing limits the visitor to just looking at the woods, as he or she might look at an animal in a zoo. It increases the feeling of separation from the natural world, rather than achieving the naturalist's goal of bringing people and nature closer together.

However, this does not preclude putting railings in dangerous spots.

The most popular way of marking interpretive spots on a trail for the visually impaired is to change the trail surface. One example would be to dig a trench across the trail and put in gravel, rather than chips or pavement. The sound and feel of the gravel underfoot will let the individual know that this is a special spot. Braille and printed brochures, tape recorders, or signs with raised letters can complete the interpretation. Since only 7 percent of visually impaired people can read braille, the tape recorder is often the best choice for them.

The State of Colorado, Division of Game, Fish and Parks, published a study of "Trails For All The People" which gives many trail ideas and designs. Their environmental design recommendations are summarized in the following chart.

DISABILITY	ENVIRONMENTAL DESIGN RECOMMENDATIONS
Amputation	Wheel chair criteria, no steep ramps, avoid steps and broken surfaces, avoid facilities requiring two handed use or great effort.
Arthritis	Provide seating for activities and easily gripped rails and handles. Avoid necessity for minute hand movements.
Blindness	Avoid physical hazards and steps where possible. Use ramps, railings, physical or audial directions and communications.
Cardio-vascular	Avoid physical environments requiring extreme exertion, i.e. steep ramps, long stairs. Place facilities within easy reach.
Cerebral palsy	Wheel chair criteria. Plan for lower mental capacity. Provide rails, seating. Eliminate hazards.
Deaf–Dumb	Visual communications must be provided.
Epilepsy	Avoid hazards. Access to assistance should be kept open at all times.
Geriatric	Wheel chair criteria. Eliminate ground and floor hazards. More frequent restrooms. All general criteria here applicable to elderly.
Mental Illness	Difficult to translate into physical requirements. Plan for elimination of potential aggravations in the environment.
Mental Retarded	Challenging, but safe physical environment needed. Simple and explicit directions with large visual graphics.
Multiple Sclerosis	Wheel chair criteria. Facilities must be planned for inevitably increasing disablement.
Muscular Dystrophy	Wheel chair criteria. Limit manipulatory items in the environment. Moving things, such as handles and latches, should be effortless.
Polio	Wheel chair criteria.

Shelters, benches, toilets, first aid, and water fountains are comforts which should be considered in the design of any area that will be used by the physically or mentally handicapped. Hazards include steep grades, poor trail surface, trails that are too long or too narrow for wheelchair maneuvering, as well as safety hazards like sharp limbs, windy areas, rock slides, and ice.

The trail surface must be usable by the narrow wheelchair wheels, which means that loose gravel and sand will not work. Paving can destroy the aesthetics of a natural area, but may be acceptable in an urban park.

Wood chips are difficult for many forms of movement, but look good on a trail. Crushed limestone works well because it packs to a good, smooth surface, but still retains drainage. It is also easy to apply and does minimal damage to the surrounding natural areas.

The types of signs and guides that are used on the trails must be adequate for the blind and mentally retarded, and benches and signs must be reachable by all trail users. In wet spots, the stepping stones which are useable and aesthetic on most trails are barriers to the handicapped.

Juggling the needs and wants of many people is difficult, but keep in mind the integrity of the natural environment. Jonathan Schwartz adds this thought:

> Many nature centers have gone out of their way to provide the visually impaired with safe trails. Many have in fact gone too far. By eliminating all the "danger," they have rendered the experience tame and lifeless. The visually impaired have, with the help of Orientation and Mobility training, mastered the streets of our busiest cities. Certainly they can handle a nature trail.

The same thought can be applied to all trails and to all people. Be aware of the environment and its carrying capacity.

Twelve

Expedition Planning

A beaver pond is so much like my mind I look into its mirror and I glimpse what lies up here behind my brows.

LOREN EISELEY

Expeditions are immersions within the natural world for extended periods of time. They usually involve research or study, travel, and the use of skills, such as backpacking, canoeing, sailing, skiing, skin diving and/or climbing.

Planning a group expedition is like a military campaign. It needs clear objectives, a plan to meet those objectives, and the supplies and equipment necessary to succeed. In addition, there is the need to anticipate and react to the emotions of both the group and the individual. A group must have good morale for a good experience. A group is made up of individuals who have their own particular needs, but it also becomes a collective entity with group moods and group needs.

The initial decision for the expedition involves its purpose. Why are you going? Are the goals physical, intellectual, psychological, or educational? Perhaps it is just curiosity. Is there an obtainable objective or is the expedition open-ended? Is the expedition being offered to make money, promote a cause, or further an educational program?

Is the expedition a wilderness trek, a geographical study, a research base camp, or a sociological study in a foreign community?

The choice of a location must conform to the purpose of the expedition. It must be close enough to the starting point so that people will not feel that the entire trip was spent in traveling to the site and back. It should be appealing enough to attract sufficient participants to cover costs. There should be enough information about the location to be used for planning. Does the area allow you to meet the purpose of your expedition? Consideration must also be given to travel budget constraints.

On a weekend-to-weekend (nine days) outing, four days is the maximum comfortable travel time. After nine days, two days per week might be added to the travel allotment.

It is much easier to plan an expedition to a certain locale if you can read up on it prior to your departure and have information readily available to assist you in planning what to bring, what to expect, and where the best places to travel are. Surprises are not always acceptable when on expedition.

Education goals must also be determined. Will you be gathering scientific, historic, or sociological information? In what manner will it be collected and recorded? Will the expedition involve a number of unique experiences not available anywhere else, or will the group be challenging themselves through distance, climbs, extremes of climate, or exposure to a variety of wildlife? Will you be investigating an ecological controversy or environmental problem, or will the group be on a purely artistic outing, hoping to record feelings and sightings on paper through the use of paints, charcoals, pencil, photography, poetry or journals? Should you attempt to map an area for future information and use, or plan a re-creation of an historic expedition to explore some of our past?

You should become aware of unique problems that may be presented by the site you have selected, and plan how you would handle certain situations if they should arise.

Determine a traveling route to and from the site, as well as alternate routes to be used to shorten traveling time, if that is a consideration. You might add places to visit, if time is available for extra exploration, or if the original planned route is inaccessible due to weather or construction work.

After you have decided on the goals for the expedition, you must determine the method whereby those goals will be achieved. The procedure you use will depend on the goals you have selected, but the following five suggestions may help you decide on the method that is best for your expedition.

1.   Base camp: everyone gathers at one specific location each evening after exploring as a group or individually each day. This method allows for more ease in daily exploration because heavy packs will not have to be taken to each study site.

2.   Continually moving group: hiking, canoeing, driving, or other motivation puts the group into a new site each night.

3.   Converging groups: sub-groups can start in different places and move towards each other to meet at a predetermined time and location.

4.   Diverging groups: sub-groups begin together and then move towards different end points.

5.   Parallel groups: sub-groups move along different paths between the same points, perhaps even converging periodically.

The equipment necessary for any expedition will depend on the study goals you have selected, as well as the location. Equipment can be divided into two separate lists: research equipment and personal equipment. The research equipment can range from a journal and pencil for recording observations, to a complete portable lab to be used at base camps or out of the vehicle while traveling to and from a variety of locations. The type of study to be done, and the extent to which it will be done in the field, will determine what kind of research equipment you bring.

Personal equipment can be divided into the following categories:

Decide whether a base camp or continual movement will best accomplish your group goals.

A decision will have to be made whether to cook or not. Will the group be satisfied with cold meals or will some meals be warm? Will warm meals be a necessity in some locations? Options for cooking include open fires, which are prohibited in some forests and parks, and are impossible options in some desert, prairie, and mountain conditions, or cook stoves, which range in size from large capacity Coleman stoves for base camp use to one burner cook stoves for extended trips. Cook stoves require the additional weight of extra fuel.

Sterno cans provide reliable heat sources for individuals. Entire meals can be planned using a Sierra Cup, allowing two days per person on a large can. Sterno is a very lightweight and individualized way to pack for a trip on a desert or into a badlands area; it minimizes water use and waste because you prepare only what you will be eating or drinking.

The following items should be included in the expedition kitchen:

1. Pots and pans (nesting type to minimize space)
2. Individual eating utensils: a cup and a spoon will take care of a backpacker's needs, along with a pocket knife. A base camp allows more amenities.
3. Dish soap and pot scrubber: use a biodegradable product (Ivory liquid)
4. Hot pot holders: base camp item
5. Rain fly: base camp protection for the kitchen
6. Matches: stored in watertight container
7. Large spoons for cooking and serving: base camp
8. Water jugs
9. Ropes for hanging packs in bear country

The Ivory liquid can be used to wash dirty dishes, dirty hands, and dirty clothes too. It should also be used to soap the bottom of the cook pots before placing them over a wood fire. The soap film will make removal of charcoal much easier at cleanup time. When applied on the first day of camp, it creates a coating on the bottom of the kettle that will protect even if the pot is used every day. It will not be necessary to scrub the pan and resoap it each day of the outing. **Warning:** Do not soap the kettle and then dip it into the water to fill. This will put the soap into the water source, as well as cause some of the soap on the kettle to run into the water inside, which could cause diarrhea. Use another, unsoaped kettle, as a dipper. Dump your dirty dishwater away from the water source, at least twenty feet from the water's edge.

Water jugs are necessary around a base camp for holding cooking water, for cleaning, and for drinking purposes. Individual water containers must also be included, especially when hiking away from a base camp or in desert or prairie areas. Plan on ¾ to 1½ gallons of water per person per day in these areas. Cooler temperatures will demand less water intake.

Two ropes are needed to suspend a food pack in bear country. The first rope is used to raise the pack from the ground and the second is used to pull the pack away from any tree trunks.

BEDROOM

The major item in an expedition bedroom is a sleeping bag that will protect the user through a variety of temperature ranges and will be a size and weight which will be appropriate for the expedition. Heavier and bulkier bags can be packed into canoes for short portages, but will add too much weight and take up too much space when backpacking.

A sleeping pad is used to prevent the cold from transferring to the sleeping bag from the ground, as well as to fill in the space between roots, rocks, and uneven ground. It should be thin and easily rolled up. Many of the products on the market will crack at temperatures below zero, so check the available equipment carefully when making selections for Arctic and sub-zero expeditions.

Shelters for expeditions come in many forms; tents are the most popular. They add protection from insects, rain, and wind, which can wick off heat from the top of the sleeping bag. They should have a low profile for the wind conditions that exist on mountains, beaches, and prairies, and should be light weight for backpacking. Large, heavy tents could be used for base camp situations and make ideal camp labs, research or storage shelters. Other options include the use of rain flies only, mosquito netting, snow caves and quinzee huts, cabins or other permanent structures.

TOILET

A campsite, whether permanent or temporary, needs a latrine arrangement. With some common sense and careful use, it is possible to establish a latrine for the camp that will not be noticeable after the group has left. Remove the top vegetation layer carefully and set it aside to be replaced on top when the camp is packed up. If the top layer is sod, use a shovel to cut a square or rectangle and then turn up an edge of the sod and roll it up, using the shovel to help separate the sod from the next soil layer. This is called scalping and can also be used to set up and repair campfire sites. After each person's use of the latrine, a shovelful of dirt should be put back into the pit. When the campsite is cleaned up, repack the hole, and replace the sod or vegetation layer.

Toilet paper is a welcome commodity. Some people prefer to just use leaves, however, you must be certain that the leaves you pick are not irritants. If you do carry toilet tissue, do not use the dyed ones, as the dyes are pollutants.

The soap that you include with your toilet items should be Ivory, which is pure soap, or one of the biodegradable bars or liquids which are available from camping and backpacking outfitters and dealers.

OFFICE

Reading materials and field guides should be distributed throughout the group to lessen the load. Books can add a lot of weight, so determine ahead of time how much you will actually need and bring only what is absolutely necessary.

Do not bring radios, tapedecks, clocks, or watches. Eliminate time as a part of your daily existence. The lack of artificial time and timepieces allows people to, in a way, become immortal. They may live in all ages at once. You can plunge into history as if you are actually there, in another time, and you may debate about the future in an atmosphere that makes the future the same as the present.

The Cheyenne Indians say that every place is made up of all things that have ever and will ever happen there. This is more than a concept of cycles, it is a concept of immortality.

A watch is a tool, but you do not need it in the wilderness. Allow yourself to experience a day without worrying about what time it is. Be attuned to your own inner clock.

Always include a map of the area and a compass in your selection of gear for an expedition. Topographic maps should be ordered well in advance of the trip and should be studied ahead of time so that you can acquaint yourself with the area that you will be traveling through. They can also aid in finding campsite locations, water sources, scientific areas, and portage routes.

Binoculars are an optional item, but they can add tremendous depth to your observations. They can also be turned over and used to view small objects up close, becoming ten power magnifiers when you look through the large end.

Other optional items include a camera and art materials, depending on the procedure you have selected for recording information.

HOSPITAL: FIRST AID SUPPLIES

1. Bandaids for small cuts and abrasions
2. Butterfly bandaids for large cuts and deep wounds
3. First aid gauze and tape
4. Antiseptic soap and ointment
5. Scalpels in sterilized containers to use for removal of tissue around puncture and foreign items which become lodged in the epidermis. Use with caution.
6. Snake bite kits (when appropriate). If danger is present and first aid is more than a day away, carry antivenin.
7. Hydrogen peroxide for removal of particles lodged in abrasions.
8. Chlor-trimetron for minor reactions to bee stings and other allergies.
9. Epinephrine for dangerous reactions to allergies and antivenin. This must be carried if antivenin is taken along, because the antivenin is a horse serum which can cause a severe reaction. This will counteract it. It requires a prescription and a doctor's advice.
10. Moleskin for blisters
11. Triangular bandage, slings and splints. Air splints can cause great damage if used improperly.
12. Aspirin and Tylenol for pain and headache
13. Lomotil (needs a prescription) for severe diarrhea which can cause dehydration, which is particularly hard to treat on a wilderness expedition.
14. Sunblock for use when traveling on glaciers and in high elevations, as well as on oceans and lakes where too much sun exposure can have serious effects.

THE GARAGE: YOUR PACK

If the expedition will be moving from place to place, group members will have to carry all of their clothing, food, water, study materials, and research items in a pack. Every designer has a list of reasons describing the benefits of their own particular brand, but the choice is strictly personal. The following list describes some of the options, not the individual brands for each kind.

Frame pack.   This is considered a reliable, well organized pack for long outings. It is designed to store the equipment in a vertical load so that the weight is carried on the hips, not the shoulder. It should fit the hiker's torso length and should be packed with the heaviest items on top.

Soft pack.   These frameless packs are for shorter outings and for skiing, when you need to have less restricted arm movement.

Duluth or Portage Packs.   These canvas bags with two leather straps are not for long hikes. They are made to fit into a canoe and for portages. The bags conform well to the bottom of the canoe and are easy to pack.

Day packs.   These are a smaller version soft pack which are handy to have when traveling away from a base camp. They are sized to hold a lunch and a few items to make the hiker comfortable. They can be packed into a larger frame pack and then be used when you do not have to carry everything.

Plastic garbage bags.   These are not packs, but are very useful pack liners. No pack is 100 % waterproof and at the end of a hard day it is a very deflating experience to unpack a soggy tent, sleeping bag, and food. Line the pack and stuff sacks with these. Then put one over your pack at night to keep it dry.

Stuff sacks.   These come in a variety of sizes and colors and can be used to separate and pack loose items, like food and clothing. They close with a draw string. Using these in your pack will cut down on your rummaging each time you need to get something out.

For bike touring, the pack goes on the bike, not on the rider. Pack all of your gear so that it does not restrict your pedaling, keep it balanced, and make sure that it is not loose or sticking into the spokes. Keep the weight as low on the bike as possible to maintain a low center of balance. This will give better control and less chance of tipping.

Keep stiff cardboard or something rigid inside your panniers to prevent bulges that will interfere with your spokes. Keep the panniers away from your heels so your pedaling is not impeded. Front packs help distribute the weight evenly and give you more sorting ability for your camp needs.

In addition to regular camping equipment, bike touring requires a lock and chain, rear carrier, panniers, handlebar bag, tool kit, tire patching kit, air pump, cycling gloves, and a helmet.

The garage is usually a storehouse for tools and maintenance, and the expedition garage must be prepared for vehicle and equipment breakdown too.

If there are a number of packs on an expedition, items like those for maintenance, first aid, and the cook kit can be distributed between them. The leader should not have to carry everything.

REPAIR KITS FOR EXPEDITIONS

Canoes. Duct tape for metal repair (seams and holes); Fiberglas repair kit for appropriate canoes and paddles; screwdriver and pliers to repair yokes, thwarts; bubblegum (when chewed and heated, bubblegum will seal holes in any canoe, especially if the hole is covered with duct tape).

Packs, tents, and sleeping bags. Extra clevis pins (multiple sizes) and slip rings; needle and thread; duct tape for large rips; nylon cord; safety pins; rip stop patches (self adhesive).

Snowshoes. Nylon cord to mend broken shoes and torn webbing; extra bindings.

Skis. Extra basket and tip for poles; Plastic ski tip; strapping tape—nylon reinforced tape for wrapping broken poles; spare binding; extra screws; epoxy.

FOOD

Because of the variety of diet preferences in any group of people, it will be almost impossible to please everyone for every meal. Try to have good food, not cheap or artificial. There are some very good freeze dried foods on the market and complete meals can be made up using these items. Do not pre-judge them just because you have heard others say they are bland. The items are improved each year and the variety is fantastic. The use of a combination of additional spices will help to satisfy even the fussiest eaters.

Some interesting menus can also be created by shopping in your local grocery. Determine how you will be traveling, whether

The meals, along with their preparation and clean-up, are often a great morale factor.

backpacking, base camping, canoeing, or whatever, and then decide the easiest way to pack the items. Canned goods can be used in some areas, but are banned in others. If carrying water will be a problem, freeze dried will not be your best choice.

Allow for extra calories because the exertion of backpacking and canoeing will burn them up much faster. Pack high energy foods for mid-morning and mid-afternoon lulls, and have a special treat packed for the middle of each week to lift spirits.

Warm food has a positive effect on group morale, even if it is just the addition of a cup of soup or hot chocolate to a cold or dry meal. Do not try to get too fancy or select items that take a long time to prepare.

After packing the food, also pack a menu for the week and stick to it. This will prevent running out of certain items, disagreements over what should be eaten, and help you stick to a varied and balanced diet.

Winter offers special problems in packing. The following items are necessary when packing for snowshoe and ski conditions.

General Equipment. Skis and poles; snowshoes; backpack; compass; map; flashlight; lantern; candles (optional); swiss army knife; monoculars (optional); journal and pencil (pencil will not freeze up); book optional: nights can be very long in the winter.

Kitchen equipment. Cook pot; Sierra cup; spoon; water bottle; matches; stove and fuel (optional); saw or hatchet.

"Bedroom" equipment. Shovel and ground cloth to prepare snow cave; tent, bivouac bag, or fly; sleeping pad; sleeping bag; vapor barrier liner (optional).

First Aid Kit. Triangular bandage; gauze and tape; ace bandage; Lomotil; aspirin or Tylenol; Erythromicin; moleskin; Bandaids; tweezer.

Vehicle Kit. Shovel; chains; towchain; charcoal and lighter fluid to warm oil pan; ether; matches.

Equipment Aid. Ski waxes; ski tip; epoxy; reinforced tape; extra d-rings; snowshoe binding; ski binding.

Clothing List; gaiters; knit hat or helmet; wool pants; wool shirts two, lightweight and heavy; wool long johns, two pair; wool socks (one pair per day, up to four pair); raincoat and rain chaps; down vest; down booties; camp boots; trail boots; extra mittens.

Gather weather data from the park or forest personnel ahead of time and know what conditions might be possible for the area in which you will be traveling. Contact the United States Weather Bureau for weather trends in the expedition site area and also contact the region's major television or radio station to ask for current conditions and projections.

Rain Gear For Canoeing: The following list was compiled by Cliff Jacobson in the April 1980 issue of *Canoe** magazine and is offered as a suggested list for preparing a canoe expedition for rain conditions.

*© Voyager Publications Inc. 1980. Reprinted with permission from April/May 1980 CANOE magazine, 131 E. Murray St., Fort Wayne, IN 46803.

Backpackers would have to cut down on weight, but the suggestions listed here include items that could be adapted to a pack.

Clothing.   Loose fitting two-piece hooded rainsuit, one size larger than normal. This aids ventilation and permits bulky clothing underneath; all-rubber boots or L. L. Bean-type rubber bottom shoe pacs; one hundred percent wool shirts and trousers; eighty-five percent wool and 15 percent nylon weaves are much less water resistant; "Scotchgard" or "Zepel" treated broad-brimmed hat of wool, felt, or canvas with chin strap; cotton/dacron or nylon-hooded wind shell (not waterproof); rubber-coated cotton gloves or buckskin gloves, wet buckskin dries soft; oiled wool sweater or heavyweight wool jacket-shirt; vest-type lifejacket, long enough to cover kidneys, which provides excellent insulation besides serving its primary lifesaving function.

For severe conditions such as icy rains, snow, and wind chills to well below freezing, add: wool longjohns; wool stocking cap; wool turtleneck sweater or Polarguard® vest; Neoprene wet suit gloves,

Winter presents new experiences—it is not the time to stay indoors.

leather-faced wool mittens; or fingerless wool "Millar mitts"; broad-brimmed Souwester-style hat with ear flaps and chin strap (optional); heavy-duty hand creme for chapped hands, and lip balm; these are essential comfort items, so do not forget them!; a large bandanna to clean glasses. Daub bandanna with insect repellent and wear around neck when traveling in buggy areas.

Canoe Gear. Fitted splash cover for canoe (optional, but once you've used one you'll never go without); eighteen-inch square piece of Ensolite® foam for kneeling in canoe and as a seat cushion in camp; waterproof map case and spare map; large natural sponge and two-quart plastic shaker for bailing, which can also be used for mixing beverages and measuring foodstuffs; moleskin to be included in your waterproof first-aid kit. Blisters are more common when feet are wet.

Drill holes in the forward and aft thwarts of the canoe and install lengths of shock-cord in each thwart. The banded thwarts will provide essential security for maps, sponge, and oddities in high winds.

Be sure to provide a skid-proof canoe bottom. The wet floor of a Royalex hull will not secure your knees when running rapids. For increased warmth and added insurance against slipping, duct-tape foam to the top of metal and plastic canoe seats.

Your gear is part of your experience, and taking proper care of it after the trip is an important part of the expedition.

Install an under-seat fold-out or thwart-mounted compass on the canoe for traveling on complex waterways. Your hands will be busy controlling your canoe in rough weather, and you will have no time to fumble through layers of clothing for your compass. Never leave a liquid-filled compass exposed to direct sunlight for extended periods of time because the capsule may explode.

Equip the canoe with twenty-foot long "painters" at each end. Under high wind conditions canoes should be securely tied to trees or boulders: never simply "pull up on shore."

Camping Items. You will need a ground sheet for inside your tent. Water which wicks through leaky tent floor seams will be trapped under the interior ground cloth. Do not put the ground sheet under the tent; rain water will be trapped between ground sheet and tent floor and be forced into the tent.

A welcome luxury in foul weather is a vestibule for your tent. It provides room to store wet boots, clothes, and packs, and seals off vulnerable door seams from the weather. It also improves the aerodynamic stability of your tent.

Other items are: Waterproof matches; butane lighter, candles; fire-ribbon or other chemical fire starter; hand axe, folding saw, heavy-duty pocket knife or thin-bladed sheath knife; gasoline stove which is the hottest and most reliable of stove fuels.

Also take a thermos bottle, keeping it filled with hot tea, Russian tea, or coffee; a ten-foot square or larger rain tarp, and carry plenty of chute cord and aluminum tent stakes for rigging; flashlight; and waterproof gear and camera bags.

Always prepare for the extremes that are possible and then you will be able to handle all weather conditions. Plan ahead of time what steps would be taken in a rain, snow or wind storm, flooding or flash flood, earthquake, rock slide, avalanche, or large waves. What will you do if the river you had intended to canoe is dry or the mountains you wanted to hike are still choked with snow?

A backup plan for weather and first aid emergencies should be set up during the trip planning and should include check points where a group could pull out in case of an emergency, locations of hospitals and police, as well as a listing of their telephone numbers, an optional end point if a group cannot make it to the planned destination, and a person who will take collect calls and be a clearing house for messages. Be prepared for lost people. Who would you contact? What would you do?

A major part of an expedition includes traveling to and from the site, and if the trip is long, who decides when toilet, stretch, and food breaks are necessary? Plan some interesting stops along the way. Visit historical sites and museums, or just stop at an area to get out and stretch. If necessary, pack food separately to be eaten while traveling.

Should a restaurant stop be planned? Sometimes this type of break can be a pleasant one in the event that storms, bad roads, or falling behind schedule makes eating packed food or having to cook out a chore rather than a pleasure.

Plan your route using the current official state maps which are available from the state highway departments, or contact The American Automobile Association (AAA) who will map a route, explain detours and problem areas, and suggest alternate routes and scenic areas.

An expedition entails a number of jobs and decisions, both in pre-trip planning and on the trip itself. Organize the group and give each participant a responsibility towards making the expedition a success.

Pre-Trip

1. Determine the purpose of the expedition
2. Select site
3. Write for information
4. Determine the study procedure to be followed
5. Make up a budget and set a cost for each participant
6. Publicize the expedition
7. Make up equipment lists
8. Make up a menu
9. Order and purchase food and supplies
10. Send a letter to each participant
11. Pack equipment

On Expedition

1. Decisions en-route
2. Camp spots, times to eat
3. Emergency situations and first aid
4. Changes in plans
5. Supervise studies
6. Organize data
7. Arbitrate personal problems
8. Interview local people

No expedition can be planned without careful consideration of a budget. One of the major costs may be the personnel involved, both in preparation time as well as actual expedition time. Include consultant's costs in your planning.

Transportation, whether traveling by car, truck, van or bus, must be figured at a mileage amount that includes vehicle cost, gas and oil consumption, and maintenance. The Federal government's business mileage allotment is low, so check with local businesses or institutions to see what they consider travel cost to be. Rental companies also have good information. Allow for extra miles in the event of emergencies, shuttles, and alterations in the route. Public transportation costs, shuttle services, and canoe, sailboat, or other travel equipment rental should also be included.

As a result of any trip use, your equipment loses some of its life, so depreciation of equipment should be figured into the budget as well. Set aside some money towards equipment replacement.

Consider food costs and lodging, including campground fees, cabins, motels, supplies to be packed, art and photo equipment, research materials, maps and first aid.

Pre-trip planning expenses consist of postage, secretarial fees, telephone, paper, and overhead. Does a facility or staff have to be maintained while the trip is in progress? What portion of that cost should be included?

Never forget a "contingencies" amount, which is a budget item that allows for the unexpected. And if your group wants to make a profit, this should be considered when preparing the budget for the expedition.

If your trip plan has to be approved or you are seeking funding, the entire expedition should be written up in the following proposal format, which also can be used as a working paper to publicize and complete your expedition.

Expedition Title:

Synopsis: (Brief description to promote the expedition)

Dates:

Sponsoring Institution:

Proposed Cost To Participants:

If Funding Proposal, Amount Requested:

Purpose of Expedition:

Significance of Project: (Why funding is desirable)

Procedure To Be Followed:

Personnel: (background and function)

Disposition and Completion of Studies:

Budget: (show where requested monies will be used)

First Aid and Weather Precautions:

Bibliography and Suggested Readings:

Appendixes: (Letters of recommendation and verification)

Follow-up: After any trip, the equipment must be repaired, cleaned or maintained. Future success of a program will depend on the care that the equipment receives.

CARE AND MAINTENANCE OF EQUIPMENT

Backpacks

1. Check all clevis pins and rings.
2. Check stitching on pack and belt.
3. Check frame for cracks.
4. Clean with water and sponge (no detergent).
5. Be sure pack is dry before storing away.
6. Tighten sweat band.

Sleeping Bag

1. Air out in good sunlight.
2. Store in hanging position or in large stuff sack or pillow case.
3. Wash in warm water with Ivory liquid or special soap for down sleeping bags. Place in bathtub or large tub and walk barefoot on it to work liquid through the bag. Rinse many times until water runs clear. Gather up (do not allow it to hang—force of weight may tear open seams) and lay it out in a sunny spot to partially dry, then place in a large clothes dryer on low heat with a tennis shoe or comparable object to maintain fluff while drying.
4. Patch holes or tears with rip-stop tape.
5. Feathers should be pushed in, rather than pulled out, if they are projecting through the fabric.
6. Packaged down may be purchased and added to the bag to restore loft.

Tents

1. Store dry.
2. Waterproof seams with commercial seam sealer annually.
3. Straighten bent poles using a vice and replace cracked and broken ones.
4. Check mosquito netting for holes or tears.
5. Check all zippers and replace if necessary.
6. Repair tears with ripstop tape.

Canoes

1. Pound out dents with a rubber mallet. Excessive pounding will weaken the metal.
2. Patch holes with fiberglas repair kit on appropriate canoes.
3. Aluminum welding must be done by a specialist.
4. Holes and breaks in aluminum canoes may be patched
   a. Secure the proper alloy and thickness of aluminum from your manufacturer.
   b. Pound out damaged area and drill ⅛ or smaller holes at each end of the tear so it will not run.
   c. Determine patch size on boat and drill rivet holes on each corner; begin by drilling only one and securing it with a bolt before proceeding to each corner and repeating operation.
   d. Put rivet holes at one inch intervals around edge.
   e. Remove bolts and patch, applying a layer of waterproof caulking (not all types will adhere to aluminum) or cementing a piece of neoprene rubber to area.
   f. Put the patch back on with bolts and begin to rivet; remove the bolts and rivet the corners as well.

Snowshoes

1. Clean and varnish snowshoe webbing and wood with a good spar varnish annually. No cheap varnish should be substituted.
2. Oil leather bindings annually.
3. Check webbing for tears, wood for cracks, and aluminum for bends and cracks.
4. Store hanging up.

Skis

1. Strip wax.
2. Pine tar wooden ski bottoms.
3. Hot wax non-wooden bottoms (wax too).
4. Check for loose screws on bindings; put a drop of epoxy in to secure screw.
5. A piece of toothpick or wooden matchstick placed into a hole will help to secure a screw if the hole becomes too large.
6. P-tex candles should be used to repair scratches and gouges on ski bottoms; remove wax first.
7. Repaint scratches on the sides of skis to keep moisture off.
8. Use epoxy to repair fiberglas that comes off of the top of a ski.
9. Store with bottoms together and a wooden block between skis to maintain camber.

Climbing Gear

1. Dry climbing ropes and webbing before storing.
2. Keep stored ropes and webbing away from direct sun and petroleum products.
3. Keep rope and webbing clean; rinse and dry if used in dirt, mud or rain.
4. Check entire length of rope and webbing for abrasions, tears, and signs of wear.
5. Look at anchors for cracks or signs of weakness.

Bibliography: The Naturalist's Library

> My chief motive, my most earnest underlying wish, has been to stop the extermination of harmless wild animals; not for their sakes, but for ours, firmly believing that each of our native wild creatures is in itself a precious heritage that we have no right to destroy or put beyond the reach of our children.
>
> ERNEST THOMPSON SETON

No one can read all of the books written, so any recommended list is dependent on those books the author has encountered. These are my favorites. There are no field guides listed because field guides are a matter of individual preference and the ones you start with and get used to will probably be the best for you.

There are field guides written on everything, sometimes unnecessarily. Birds, mammals, mammal tracks, trees, wildflowers, ferns, butterflies, bird nests, reptiles and amphibians are all good subjects for field guides, but insects and rocks are not. The layperson that picks up a rock and tries to flip through 350 pages of rock pictures in an attempt to identify it will become very frustrated. The insect hunter who looks for one out of 990,000 insects will be exhausted. Insect guides have to be by order to be helpful, and good luck to that guide writer.

It is a good idea to build your working library around your particular region. Many of the books I use for geology, and flora and fauna, are not on the following list because they are too specific to my area, but in my teaching, localized information is most pertinent. The people I instruct may never view the examples in a book of national scope, but they will see the drumlin in their own backyard.

PHILOSOPHY

Walden, Henry David Thoreau, New American Library, New York, 1960. This book is a classic in wilderness ethic. Thoreau's theme of morning is clearly an expression of his spiritual reverence for nature. He wrote, "Every morning was a cheerful invitation to make my life of equal simplicity, and I may say innocence, with Nature herself. I have been as sincere a worshipper of Aurora as the Greeks. I got up early and bathed in the pond; that was a religious exercise, and one of the best things which I did." This is a book devoted to looking closer. Use Thoreau's description of the ants as an inspiration for your own observations and writing.

The Night Country, Eisley Loren, Scribner's, New York, 1971. This is a light book written by a man who has found some kinship with the world. He is an anthropologist who takes you into the sewer and lets you observe from new perspectives. "The terror that confronts our age is our own conception of ourselves. Above all else this is the potion which the modern Dr. Jekylls have concocted."

A Sand County Almanac, Aldo Leopold, Oxford University Press, London, 1949. Leopold shaped an ethic from the sand that strained through his fingers, and modern game management developed from it. This book is a seasonal diary of his observations on a Wisconsin sand plain and it it filled with love and insight. "The rough-leg has no opinion why grass grows, but he is well aware that snow melts in order that hawks may again catch mice. He came down out of the Arctic in the hope of thaws, for to him a thaw means freedom from want and fear."

How to Talk to Birds, Richard C. Davids, Knopf, New York, 1972. The author's pleasure in natural things flows from the book like an inspiration. Why raise moths in your living room? Because that is where you are and they are beautiful. "But to me it is a purposeful evolution, with a God in charge, a God with a sense of humor. The feeling grows stronger every time I encounter a little spicebush larva, with his mark of the whimsy of God on him. I am again aware of God's sense of humor when I visit the zoo, and even more so when I visit an aquarium. The garishly decorated parrot fish are as overdecorated as a dance-hall hostess of the 1890's. Such a view, scientific purists will say, is a hopeless conceit. Nature was not put on earth to please and amuse mankind. But perhaps to a thoughtful parrot fish or a sensate spicebush swallowtail, man offers a few light moments in return."

The Sense of Wonder, Rachel Carson, Harper & Row, New York, 1956. This is a sensitive book by a woman who felt the cries of anguish from nature itself. She awoke a nation with *Silent Spring* and, in this text, which she was working on when she died, she has inspired us to reach out and share a sense of wonder with our children. In describing the night sky, she wrote, "It occurred to me that if this were a sight that could be seen only once a century or even once in a human generation, this little headland would be thronged with spectators. But it can be seen many scores of nights in any year, and so the lights burned in the cottages and the inhabitants probably gave not a thought to the beauty overhead; and because they could see it almost any night, perhaps they will never see it."

Reflections from the North Country, Sigurd Olson, Knopf, New York, 1976. No book addresses itself to the solitude and timelessness of wilderness more than this collection of essays by America's premier canoeist-naturalist. It is a book that looks back on many years of experience and bridges the gap between voyageur and canoe vacationist. Sigurd Olson is the true voice of the canoe country along the Canadian border. "I know now as men accept the time clock of the wilderness, their lives become entirely different. It is one of the great compensations of primitive experience, and when one finally reaches the point where days are governed by daylight and dark, rather than by schedule, where one eats if hungry and sleeps when tired, and becomes completely immersed in the ancient rhythms, then one begins to live."

PICTURE BOOKS TO READ

The High West, Les Blacklock and Andy Russell, Viking, New York, 1974. Magnificent pictures and moving script to capture the mood of the mountains.

The Hidden Forest, Les Blacklock and Sigurd Olson, Viking, New York, 1969. This book reveals the essence of the canoe country by two men who have been moved by its beauty.

The Living World of Audubon, Ronald Clement, Grosset and Dunlap, New York, 1974. Audubon's art takes on a new dimension when coupled with great photographs.

John Muir's Longest Walk, John Earl, Doubleday, Garden City, New York, 1975. John Muir formulated his philosophy during this walk. The excerpts from his notes and the photographs give insight into the mind of this great naturalist.

North America and the Great Ice Age, Charles Matsch, McGraw-Hill, New York, 1976. This is a most readable and informative text on this major geological phenomenon.

Living Earth, Peter Farb, Harper & Row, New York, 1959. Soils and the mysterious creatures of the organic levels can be fun.

Environmental Geology, Peter Flawn, Harper & Row, New York, 1970. This puts it all together. Don't fight the earth. Understand its geology and use sensible land use planning. This is practical geology.

Pond Life, George Reid, PhD, Golden Press, New York, 1967. This Little Golden Book is the best of the series. It is a gold mine of practical information.

Stalking The Wild Asparagus, Euell Gibbons, David McKay Company, Inc., New York, 1962. This was the leader in wild foods and this is the best of his books. It is not a field guide, it does not have all the possible plants listed, and it does not have all the recipes, but it is fun to read and the recipes given are good. It is a nice way to start.

How Indians Use Wild Plants For Food, Medicine And Crafts, Frances Densmore, Dover, New York, 1928. This reprint is a classic work on the Indian use of native plants. The Ojibway Indians were the subject of the study done by the Bureau of Ethnology. I enjoyed it even before I found out that my great-great-grandmother was one of the informants for the text. It overflows with information.

Forests of Lilliput, John Bland, Prentice-Hall, Englewood Cliffs, New Jersey, 1971. This is the most enjoyable plunge into the world of lichens and mosses that I have ever made.

Prairie Plants and Their Environment, J.E. Weaver, University of Nebraska Press, Lincoln, Nebraska, 1968. Grasses are our most important plant if we think of economic benefit. They are a part of the heritage of our western movement and the agricultural pioneers. They are also a source of beauty. This book explores the complexities of the grassland environment.

The Habitat Guide To Birding, Thomas McElroy, Jr., Knopf, New Jersey, 1974. This is the total approach to birding. Birds are not apart from ecology—they are part of it and should be studied as such.

Mammals of North America, Victor Cahalane, MacMillan, New York, 1968. You not only get the facts you want about the mammal, but you also get a lot of enjoyable reading.

The Tracker, Tom Brown and William Watkins, Prentice-Hall, Englewood Cliffs, New Jersey, 1978. This book is an adventure story and the most inspiring treatise on tracking I have ever read. It makes the reader want to look for the first available track and follow it forever. The ideas for activities involving tracking are endless.

The Complete Walker, Colin Fletcher, Knopf, New York, 1968. The good sense and attitude of this book on backpacking applies to many other outdoor sports. It is also fun reading.

Roughing It Easy, Dian Thomas, Brigham Young University Press, Provo, Utah, 1974. Make cooking fun and part of your outdoor experience. Wild foods add one dimension to outdoor eating and this adds another.

Be An Expert With Map and Compass, Bjorn Kjellstrom, Charles Scribner's Sons, New York, 1976. Bjorn Kjellstrom's name is becoming an eponym for orienteering. There is no greater expert.

Medicine For Mountaineering, James Wilkerson, MD, The Mountaineers, Seattle, Washington, 1975. The most authoritative guide to practical first aid for the expedition and field.

KIDS' BOOKS THAT ADULTS SHOULD READ

Natural Partnerships, Dorothy Shuttlesworth, Doubleday, Garden City, New York, 1969. This is a well illustrated description of symbiosis. Good for fifth and sixth graders.

Animal Camouflage, Dorothy Shuttlesworth, The Natural History Press, Garden City, New York, 1966. This text is written for grades 4–6, but the illustrations are good for all grades.

hope for the flowers, Trina Paulus, Paulist Press, New York, 1972. This book is an illustration of a lifestyle. It is the tale of a caterpillar that is fun reading for third graders, and even more fun and thought provoking for adults.

The Beaver Pond, Alvin Tresselt, Lothrop, Lee and Shepard Company, New York, 1970. A second grader can read this book and only kids up to age 101 should! The layout of the book makes it appear to be a young reader's book, and it is, but the text and treatment of the life cycle of a beaver pond is outstanding. This one is a must.

The Mountain, Peter Parnell, Doubleday, New York, 1971. This book is not for kids. The style misleads you. It is definitely an adult book. The conflict in values that this book deals with is too profound for a child to grasp, but I have had many adults read it and it is a powerful presentation for them. The illustrations are amazingly detailed and new features seem to pop up with each viewing. This is an absolute must for your library and should be left out for everyone to see.

The Bear's Nature Guide, Stan and Jan Berenstein, Random

House, New York, 1975. Do not start leading groups until you have read this. It is simplicity and effectiveness at its very best.

BOOKS FOR THE NATURALIST

The Amateur Naturalist's Handbook, Vinson Brown, Prentice-Hall, Englewood Cliffs, New Jersey, 1981.

The Curious Naturalist, John Mitchell, Prentice-Hall, Englewood Cliffs, New Jersey, 1981.

The Natural History Guide, H. Charles Laun, Alsace Books and Films, Alton, Illinois, 1970. Ideas, what to make, what to do. Excellent reference.

Nature in Miniature, Richard Headstrom, Knopf, New York, 1968. The year is placed in a calendar perspective and each month gives you clues of small things to look for and be amazed by.

Field Book of Natural History, E. Laurence Palmer, McGraw Hill, New York, 1949. This is an amazing attempt to catalog natural history knowledge. If you have just a short time to look something up, this is the book to turn to.

Handbook Of Nature-Study, Anna Botsford Comstock, Comstock Publishing, Ithaca, New York, 1919. Cornell Press is reprinting this classic work. Stories and information leap off the pages. The style is pure 1900 and will probably give you some laughs in itself, but keep reading and you will get a powerful amount of information. Old books are particularly good for giving details. They assume a less proficient background in their readers than many modern books and, consequently, the little things you assumed or wondered about are often discussed.

BOOKS FOR PLANNING EXPEDITIONS

Natural Regions of the United States and Canada, Charles Hunt, W.H. Freeman and Company, San Francisco, 1967.

The National Parks, Freeman Tilden, Knopf, New York, 1968.

Wilderness Areas of North America, Ann and Myron Sutton, Funk and Wagnalls, New York, 1974.

Guide to National Wildlife Refuges, Laura and William Riley, Anchor Press, Doubleday, Garden City, N.Y., 1979.

Wild Rivers of North America, Michael Jenkinson, Dutton, New York, 1973.